WALTER HINES PAGE AND **THE WORLD'S WORK**

1900-1913

Robert J. Rusnak
Rosary College

UNIVERSITY
PRESS OF
AMERICA

Copyright © 1982 by
University Press of America,Inc.
P.O. Box 19101, Washington, D.C. 20036

Printed in the United States of America

Library of Congress Cataloging in Publication Data

Rusnak, Robert J.
    Walter Hines Page and the World's work, 1900-1913.

    Bibliography: p.
    1. Page, Walter Hines, 1855-1918. 2. World's work
(New York, N.Y.) 3. Progressivism (United States
politics) I. Title.
E664.P15R87 1982   973.8'092'4   81-40929
ISBN 0-8191-2604-7
ISBN 0-8191-2605-5 (pbk.)

093701

To Martha

TABLE OF CONTENTS

INTRODUCTION. vii

I. WALTER HINES PAGE: THE DEVELOPMENT
OF AN EDITOR. 1

II. THE FORMATION OF DOUBLEDAY, PAGE
& COMPANY AND THE WORLD"S WORK. 25

III. THE POLICIES AND CONTENTS OF
THE WORLD'S WORK: 1900-1913. 41

IV. WALTER HINES PAGE AND THE PROBLEM
OF THE "NEW IMMIGRATION": THE
PROGRESSIVE AS RACIST 75

V. WALTER HINES PAGE AND THE PROBLEM
OF NEGRO IMPROVEMENT. 105

VI. WALTER HINES PAGE AND THE "LABOR PROBLEM":
THE DILEMMA OF A MORAL PROGRESSIVE. 117

BIBLIOGRAPHY. 135

INTRODUCTION

> There was distinction in the journals
> of the new century, but it was to be
> found along the byroads rather than
> on the broad highways. The opening
> year of the century saw the establish-
> ment of The World's Work, under the
> editorship of the progressive and
> dynamic Walter Hines Page, who thus
> early revealed the awareness of Amer-
> ican responsibility in world affairs
> that was to distinguish his subsequent
> diplomatic career. He had served an
> apprenticeship on the querulous Forum
> and the sedate Atlantic and was thus
> familiar with the best traditions of
> the older journalism and initiated
> into the practices of the newer. His
> own preference was for a liberalism
> that was lively without being sensa-
> tional, an internationalism that was
> responsible but not imperialistic,
> and literary standards that were
> respectable without being formidable.
> For a decade he made The World's Work
> a force of enlightenment.[1]

The purpose of this study is two-fold. First, it
presents the history of the magazine, The World's Work,
and its ideological position on the topics of immigration, race and labor. Secondly, it attempts to shed
additional light on the character and values of the
magazine's editor, Walter Hines Page. To a large degree, these purposes are complementary.

A close correlation between the magazine and the
man exists because Walter Hines Page had virtually complete control over the editorial content of The World's
Work from 1900 to 1913. The editorial pages stand
forth as clear expositions of the political, social and
economic thought of the man who became Ambassador to
the Court of St. James's under President Woodrow Wilson.

Not only the editorials, but also the articles
which appeared in The World's Work required Page's
approval. Page solicited most of the articles he
printed, and even went so far as to indicate to his

potential authors what he wanted them to include in their articles.[2] The purpose of this study, then, is to follow the development of Walter Hines Page as an editor, and to examine, through his statements in and direction of The World's Work, his public attitudes on controversial topics.

There are several secondary benefits which accrue from this approach. By limiting the topics on which in-depth analysis is made, the conservative side of the Progressive mind can be more clearly seen. In this study, analysis of the treatment of immigration, race and labor by The World's Work highlights the negative side of nationalism, democracy and business economics. The choice of immigration, race and labor as topics for discussion is not intended to ridicule Progressive thought. Rather, it is simply a method of gaining a different perspective on the multi-faceted Progressive movement.

Other studies have labeled Progressivism as a defensive rather than a positive reform movement.[3] At the very least, a close study of Progressive thought reveals doctrinal inconsistencies. Some of these in-consistencies are apparent in the public statements of Walter Hines Page, whose own outlook and beliefs re-mained constant, even in the face of social change. Actually, a certain sympathy appends to Page when one follows his personal struggles to reconcile his estab-lished beliefs to changing social conditions.

Finally, in discussing the development and success of The World's Work as a current issue magazine, we must make certain assumptions. The primary assumption is that the magazine, because of the nature of its content, had influence on people in high political and economic positions. One indication of the truth of this assumption is the appearance of such authors as William Howard Taft, Woodrow Wilson, Andrew Carnegie, James J. Hill and John D. Rockefeller in the pages of The World's Work. Also, in the words of Frank Luther Mott, the foremost historian of American magazines, "the attitudes projected by a periodical acknowledged to have been important are worthy of analysis."[4]

A second important assumption of this study is that magazines, because of their particular format, have an impact on the reading public.

Subjectively, the existence of

> magazine impact is acknowledged.
> A given periodical does have dis-
> tinctive characteristics and does
> awaken particular responses in its
> readers. Objectively, impact is
> difficult to prove, difficult even
> to describe. Some 'impact' is
> measurable; most of it is not.[5]

In addition to the appeal of its content, The World's Work had another important attribute. Page insisted upon having a well-written magazine. A writer of great force and clarity himself, he continually lamented the dearth of experts who could write. Often he returned long, learned manuscripts to their authors with the plea that they be made short and interesting. There was also, in his view, a shortage of good professional staff writers. "I should undertake," he stated in 1902, "to make a better magazine than you have ever seen, if I could find writers who could write well enough about contemporaneous things."[6] Page, however, understood the changes in the magazine world, and by dint of his imagination, editorial experience and hard work, created a thriving magazine.

For thirteen of its thirty-two year existence, Walter Page directed the destiny of The World's Work. Its immediate success, from the first issue in November, 1900, was due in great part to his capacity to blend new concepts and traditional values. On the whole, he edited the magazine to reflect his personal beliefs rather than attempting to conform to shifting public tastes. To be sure, he was circumspect in some areas, but sooner or later, he presented almost every aspect of American life as he saw it. His few topical omissions can be credited to good taste, and to the fact that magazine publishing is a business as well as an art. Few magazines which constantly offended their readers ever survive.

In his editorial presentations, Page was often unblushingly didactic. However, he viewed magazine publishing as a public service, and his editorials, even when discussing topics dear to his heart, were invariably in the public interest. Within the restrictions of the publishing world, Page was as honest as an editor could be. His honesty makes a study of his public writings especially useful in understanding the many intellectual currents of the Progressive era.

In the complex world of Progressive thought, Page and The World's Work occupied the middle ground, standing between the radical elements and the older conservative trends. A synthesis of these forces took place in the administration of Woodrow Wilson, but little heretofore has been written to show how far back this synthesis goes. Page represented, in his personal and editorial viewpoint, the Wilsonian synthesis from the first issue of The World's Work. Indeed, elements of Wilsonian Progressivism, in Page's thought and writing, extend back to the 1880's. He was always true to the values of his youth, the values of the 19th Century, but he tried, as an editor, to find a middle path between his dedication to individualism and his cognizance of current social conditions. As seen through topical analysis, Page and The World's Work reflect the doctrinal inconsistencies inherent in his unwavering belief in democratic individualism.

FOOTNOTES
INTRODUCTION

[1]Henry Steele Commager, The American Mind: An Interpretation (New Haven, 1950), p. 80.

[2]Burton J. Hendrick, The Training of an American (New York, 1928), pp. 207-208.

[3]For example: Otis L. Graham, Jr., An Encore for Reform (New York, 1967).

[4]Frank Luther Mott, A History of American Magazines. (Cambridge, Massachusetts, 1939), 1, 4-5.

[5]James Playsted Wood, Magazines in the United States, 2nd edition (New York, 1956), p. 308.

[6]Walter Hines Page, Address to the American Library Association, 1902. Reprinted in The World's Work, IV (October, 1902), 2562-63.

CHAPTER I

WALTER HINES PAGE:
THE DEVELOPMENT OF AN EDITOR

Walter Hines Page was born in Cary, North
Carolina, the son of Allison Francis (Frank) Page and
Catherine Frances Raboteau. On his father's side, the
family record dated from at least 1778, when the
Lunenburg County, Virginia records reflect the marriage
of Lewis Page, Walter's great grandfather. His
mother's family occupied and named Barclaysville,
between Fayetteville and Raleigh, in the early 1800's.
Walter was the third child born to Frank and Catherine,
the first to live, and the oldest of a group which
Josephus Daniels has described as "a family of rare
gifts". Allison F. Page, successful in the lumber and
turpentine business, had just relocated near Raleigh
when Walter Hines Page was born, on August 15, 1855.
"A.F. Page was the best type of the lumber kings in
the South, but he was much more than that. He was an
upstanding man of positive convictions and high character." He was a Methodist and a temperance man, and in
fact felt so strongly about liquor that he had included
in the charter of Cary a provision that intoxicants
never be sold in that town. The name Cary itself comes
from a celebrated prohibitionist from Ohio.[1]

Catherine Raboteau Page had received a better
education than most girls of her day, and was a reader
of good books.[2] Walter had her to himself for four
years, and even other children did not totally interfere. For lack of near-by schools, Walter's basic
education in reading, writing and mathematics came from
his mother. He never saw a school room until he was
ten years old. She was a good mother to more than one
child, as in later years, Walter Page's four brothers
proved to be substantial citizens of their state.

Henry A. Page became a railroad president and
legislator; also Food Commissioner in World War I.
Junius R. Page was the president of the Page Trust
Company and a pioneer in peach growing. Robert N. Page
served as a United States Congressman, and Frank Page
was the State Highway Commissioner responsible for the
development of good roads in North Carolina.[3] Indeed,
it was a family of rare gifts, and one whose material
fortune sprang from the efforts of Frank Page, their

father, in lumbering and railroad building.

Walter Page's first "formal" schooling took place in a log school house, operated by Adolphus Jones, a graduate of the University of North Carolina. From his tenth to his thirteenth year, Walter Page studied here winter and summer. He was a studious boy, not at all interested in physical labor. His high academic aptitude and his serious attitude led his parents to believe that he "had been set aside by the Lord for the ministry....To see the boy bestowed in a Methodist pulpit was evidently to be the great solace of their declining years." Accordingly, Walter went off to Bingham School at Mebane, North Carolina for further education. Here, he spent two years, returning to a newly opened academy at Cary, North Carolina, in 1870 for his last year of preparation.[4]

In the fall of 1871, Frank Page took Walter to enroll in Trinity College, the only Methodist college in North Carolina. Trinity later became Duke University, large and well-endowed, but in 1871, its facilities consisted of one brick building. Walter was not happy at Trinity, an unhappiness ascribed to "bleak... surroundings...too primitive...the associations, with the exception of two or three close friends, uncongenial." Page himself reported that he was learning little more than he already knew. When Reverend James A. Duncan, President of Randolph-Macon College, visited Trinity, his address inspired several Trinitarians, among them Walter Page, to transfer to the college at Ashland, Virginia.[5]

The years between January 1873 and June 1876 opened new vistas for Page. Randolph-Macon, while strongly religious in its education approach, had a faculty far superior to that at Trinity. Here, Page was exposed to men who thought in broad terms, rejecting localism for a national viewpoint. Page and his close friends read Jefferson and Madison's works "as a diversion--the kind of diversion that is one's main matter of life." Aware of the obnoxious aspects of Reconstruction, they sought a grander, if older conception of the South's role in American life.[6]

The rejection of the recent Southern experience was not difficult for Page. From his grandfather, Anderson Page, Walter had acquired a sense of the importance of the South in building the New Nation. He had already accepted the "large-minded" South of his grandfather, whose youth encompassed the 1790-1830 period of Southern domination in the Union.[7]

Among the faculty at Randolph-Macon was a man who was to have a profound effect upon Page's future. This was Thomas Randolph Price, Professor of Greek and English. Page first attracted Price's attention through his own excellence in Greek. "A young scholar of extraordinary promise," recorded Price.[8] Price invited Page, along with four or five other promising students, for personal discussions. Price's own love was the English language, "the greatest of all languages...the author who overtopped all...was Shakespeare." Burton Hendrick, Walter Page's biographer, insists that "Price taught Page to love not only the English language and English literature; above all he taught him to love England itself." Whether or not this is true remains unclear.[9]

It is true, however, that Price helped Page's academic career. Price was responsible for Page's fellowship to the newly opened Johns Hopkins graduate school, as one of the first twenty to be admitted. Page's own accomplishments in his closing year at Randolph-Macon included the Walton prize in Greek and the Sutherlin medal in oratory. Obviously, under the stimulation of a scholarly faculty, Page's latent ability was developed.

At Johns Hopkins, Page studied under Basil Gildersleeve. He found himself deficient in his preparation for Greek classics, but greatly enjoyed the life and the community, at least during his first few months.[10] However, as early as the end of November, 1876, Page had doubts about both his ability and interest in Greek scholarship. "I have a strong mind at times," he wrote, "to throw up all my scholarly plans, and go to work, go among men, I mean--go into politics, for example. Active work is worth tenfold more than book speculation. But...there is time enough in the future for that."[11]

Page spent the summer of 1877 in Germany, for travel and scholarship.[12] He returned in the fall of 1877 to Johns Hopkins, increasingly dissatisfied with himself, because he found himself working only for his own expansion and enjoyment,

> not to find out any new grammatical fact,
> nor prepare myself to teach Greek....I

manage to steal much time to read generally
in fine literature...Tennyson...Shelley,
too...I am going to begin on Italian now.
I have joined a class to read Dante....I
have not a little that is less pleasant...
I must read for grammar's sake sometimes
and get up dry statistics from dry Greek
because I hold a place whose work is just
that. In strict truth, I ought not to
hold the place I do here.[13]

In March of 1878, at the end of the term, Walter
Page left Johns Hopkins. He returned to his grandfather's farm at Crabtree to "spend...time...in
meditating on the future."[14] Shortly thereafter, he
received an invitation to teach at the newly recon-
stituted University of North Carolina's summer normal
school. For six weeks, in the summer of 1878, Page
lectured on Greek culture and English literature,
entertaining hopes of a regular appointment to the
faculty. Unfortunately, the University was too poor to
add to its already underpaid staff.

Burton Hendrick maintains that "Page had fixed
upon his life program...by this time...his ambition
was to become a leader in periodical literature."[15]
It is, however, not at all clear that this was the case.
Frank Page's economic enterprises had grown, and while
Walter Page's ambitions did not seem to lie in direct
business activity, this avenue was at least open to
him. His acceptance of a teaching position, in the fall
of 1878, at the Male Highschool in Louisville,
Kentucky, indicates further uncertainty in his career
goals. The job paid $1500.00 a year, an excellent
salary, and Page felt then that "It may open the way
for me to--well, to journalism." One semester of the
routine of teaching high school convinced him that this
was not his choice of a future, although the life in
Louisville appealed to him.[16]

In January of 1879, an opportunity to engage in
journalism appeared. The Age, modeled after the
New York Nation, became available for part purchase.
As a contributor of articles and book reviews, Page
had earlier become acquainted with the proprietors.
The Age was failing financially, but Page believed he
could pull it out. Investing $1000 that he did not
have, Page spent a hard winter as editor and half owner
before acknowledging defeat at the hands of Southern
disinterest.

The failure of The Age left Page again unemployed. He sought employment of a journalistic nature by canvassing newspapers in North Carolina, where he hoped that active journalism might lead to reform, and as far away as Baltimore and Louisville. During this period of inactivity, Page wrote and submitted to the Atlantic Monthly a piece entitled "An Old Southern Borough". His description of the narrowly religious "worship of ancient Gods...prejudice against a universal and uniform system of schools", and the general refusal to acknowledge that the "old order had passed" was accepted by the Atlantic's editor, William Dean Howells.[17]

This modest but important literary success helped to solidify Page's desire for a career in journalism. Still, he reconsidered briefly the occupation which would have been his parents fondest hope; the ministry. For Page, however, conventional religion was always lacking. In a letter to his future wife, Willa Alice Wilson, he expressed a lack of belief in the divinity and godhood of Christ, and expressed an interest in Unitarianism. However, Page's desire to preach, later to be expressed in other ways, was quickly suppressed, as Unitarianism in Raleigh would have been a personal disaster and a grave disappointment to Page's mother.

Finally, Page's far-flung advertising of his talents and availability paid off. Because hundreds of newspapers to which he sent his qualifications had ignored him, he advertised in the New York Nation as "A journalist of experience...a scholar of thorough and special university training...experienced as an editor...European correspondent...to the magazines, the Atlantic, etc..."[18]

The advertisement was answered by Mr. James Burnes, editor of the St. Joseph, Missouri Gazette. Page accepted the proffered offer in February, 1880, becoming the Gazette's stockyards reporter at a salary of $15 a week "with such opportunities of advancement as his abilities might justify." He soon moved through police reporting to "more important and dignified tasks." Five months after joining the Gazette, Page found himself in the position of Editor-in-Chief. He was exceedingly pleased with his position, despite the hard work.[19]

Prior to leaving Cary, North Carolina, in the late winter of 1880, Page became engaged to Willa Wilson whom he first met while attending the Cary Academy in preparation for Trinity. After an absence from North Carolina, Willa returned in 1877 from Michigan and renewed her acquaintance with Page during the Summer Normal school session in the summer of 1878. Once Page had established himself, even at low salary, in St. Joseph, Missouri, they were married in St. Louis, on November 15, 1880.

Page and his new bride spent the ensuing year and a half in St. Joseph, with Page generally "learning his trade."[20] He desired, however, to tour the South, study the problems, and offer the results to the American people. He proposed to write articles which would be published simultaneously in a number of newspapers. This early syndicate plan was risky, because Page was unknown to most Northern newspaper editors. However, the newspapers to which he sent his articles, among them the New York World and the Boston Post, published the articles he submitted and asked for more.

Page's personal syndicate was lucrative, but its real purpose was to lead toward a more permanent niche in journalism. Page's articles elicited such a position on the New York World, which on the strength of his letters from the South, offered him a staff job in the late summer of 1881. He accepted, but was soon traveling again, this time to "Utah to inspect at first hand the behavior of the Mormons." He also traveled, as correspondent for the World, with the tariff commission of 1882, a data collection agency to promote "scientific principles" in the setting of tariffs. Page, as a free-trader, wrote rather unsympathetically of the commission's efforts, viewing the proceedings "as an attempt of the protected interests to settle themselves permanently in power." In Atlanta, Georgia, while accompanying the tariff commission, Page first met Woodrow Wilson, then working in a law office with Edward Renick, an old friend of Page.[21]

Page stayed on the staff of the New York World until May of 1883 as a literary critic and editorial writer. When the newspaper was sold to Joseph Pulitzer, the entire staff of the World, then known as the "most genial club in the metropolis," walked out.[22]

Now twenty-eight, with a wife and two sons, Page sought a permanent place to utilize his well developed journalistic talents. His old desire to serve his state, to help in the reconciliation of North and South, and to benefit the South generally, reasserted itself.

With his family, in the autumn of 1883, Page returned to North Carolina.

Page believed that he was ready to undertake the editing of his own newspaper, a vehicle through which he could express himself and educate his beloved state of North Carolina. But his return from the activity of New York to the relatively slow and backward state of North Carolina was a shock. It was like "another world....yet a frontier....Here was poverty--a depressed population, the idle squalor of the Negro...and... hopeless inertia..." However, "they had once bred men; they shall breed men again."[23]

Almost immediately, Page took over the defunct State Chronicle in Raleigh, operating from a barren basement. His father and a few friends funded this enterprise. In form, the State Chronicle was patterned after the New York World. "It was well written on both the news and editorial pages," because Page wrote most of it himself. He began at once the task of remaking the attitudes of North Carolina, utilizing the double-edged sword of ridicule. Even though the paper pursued the non-controversial theme of development of the state's resources, Page could not resist attacking the public dedication to the old Southern shibboleths. He pointed out that there could be no progress unless the "old subject", the Negro, ceased to dominate the public mind. "North Carolina had never before been so angered, so jarred, so instructed, so entertained---all in a newspaper that was a model of neatness and good taste, written in English that was scholarly, clear and dig-nified even when most annihilating."[24]

In Page's view, the hope of North Carolina, indeed, the hope of the South, lay in the young men. New ideas, and new men unhampered by the worship of the lost cause, would lead the way in making North Carolina really re-enter the Union. A building up of the indus-trial and educational facilities of the state would in turn lead to economic prosperity and political revi-talization. This hope was shared by other young men, some of whom gravitated to Page.

The formation of the Watauga Club, in May of 1884, brought some of the best minds in the state together in an effort "to encourage free discussion and to promote the educational, agricultural and industrial interests of the state." The weight of local prejudice was such that the club assumed a non-political demeanor to avoid being labeled as too progressive. Even the name, Watauga, was chosen for its unfamiliarity. It refers to an earlier Watauga Association, named for a river in western North Carolina. The original Watauga Association was the governmental body of a group of pioneers who did not know if they belonged to Virginia or North Carolina. This group sought recognition from the new U.S. government, first as the Washington district, then as the State of Franklin, and finally succeeded in becoming the territory of Tennessee. The name, Watauga, had meaning for the club members in 1884, who felt that they too were struggling to "build out of chaos a new state..."[25] It was definitely a service club, meeting approximately once a week for discussion, especially of state problems. The State Chronicle became its unofficial organ. Its primary purpose was to:

> Widen the opportunities of the common
> man--that was the idea that dominated
> all others. Teach him modern agri-
> culture and the industrial arts; train
> him to be an expert manual labourer--
> a carpenter, a brick mason, an engineer,
> a technical mechanic; educate the picked
> sons in the higher branches and train
> the qualified for the professions;
> develop the resources of the State and
> stimulate its manufacturers, so that
> it may no longer be dependent upon the
> North for all articles of daily use,
> from cradles to coffins. Train not
> only the North Carolina boy but the
> North Carolina girl; and--more radical
> doctrine still--train the Negro.[26]

During Page's short tenure in North Carolina, the Watauga Club's major project was the establishment of industrial education in the schools of North Carolina. In early 1885, the club memorialized the legislature "To establish an industrial school in North Carolina, which shall be a training place for young men who wish to acquire skill in the wealth-producing arts and sciences."[27]

The legislature responded by passing "An Act to Establish and Maintain an Industrial School," which authorized the State Agriculture Department to seek pro-posals for its establishment in whatever town or city offered the greatest inducement. Raleigh made the best offer, that of $5000 and twenty acres of land. However, because these provisions were inadequate for the establishment of a proper school, the Watauga Club continued its agitation for wider support. The supporters of industrial education also broadened their purpose. They soon moved to make it an Agricultural and Mechanical College of North Carolina, and a bill to that effect was gotten through the legislature in March of 1877. The bill provided for State support both through general fund appropriation and bond issue, backed by the Land Script fund formerly belonging to the University of North Carolina. While the Watauga Club, during Page's membership, continued to work for the State, the Agricultural and Mechanical College was its first and finest contribution.[28]

Page, however, had left North Carolina before the educational creation of the Watauga Club opened in 1889. His newspaper had become a losing proposition, despite its success "in starting the community thinking in new directions..."[29] While this failure is ascribed by Burton Hendrick to lack of receptivity by the readership of the state, it is more probably due to Page's attempt to publish a daily instead of a weekly newspaper in Raleigh, where two other more powerful dailies were in operation. Page had hoped to get the state printing contract, "but Page was no politician, not even a general mixer, and he did not win..." the printing contract. Page tried to return to weekly publication, but finally gave up and accepted a position on the Brooklyn Union. "He turned over his interest in the paper to F.B. Arendell and went to New York, regretfully surrendering his bright dream of publishing a liberal paper in his native State."[30]

Page left North Carolina in February, 1885, as financially impoverished as when he had arrived, only two years earlier. North Carolina, even in 1883, was not prepared to accept the "New South" concept of education and industrialization. Page vented his wrath in a series of letters, known as the "Mummy" letters, which were published in his old newspaper by its new editor, Josephus Daniels, from February to April of 1886. According to Daniels: "The letters were fresh and interesting.... He pleased many and offended others, particularly by his criticism of preachers...I did not sympathize with his strictures. I was glad to print anything he wrote."[31]

The letters began in October of 1885, "dealing mainly with national affairs...[and] civil service

reform." A few "barbed paragraphs" warned of what was
to come in the spring of 1886.[32] Page likened North
Carolina society to a "mummified community, a political
and social Thothmes II--into whose dead body it was his
mission to breathe the breath of life."[33] Thothmes II
first appeared in the State Chronicle while Page was
still editor. "Page referred to a public officer who
was distinguished for his dignity and his family tree,
but not noted for any animated administration of his
duties, as 'Thothmes II'. When this bewildered func-
tionary...learned that Thothmes II was an Egyptian
King, whose dessicated mummy had recently been disin-
terred...he naturally stopped his subscription to the
paper."[34]

From his new position in New York, Page continued
to attack the three ghosts which he believed were
strangling North Carolina and the rest of the South;
the ghost of the Confederate dead, the ghost of religious orthodoxy, and the ghost of Negro domination.[35]
The fact that he accomplished no significant change in
North Carolina attitudes, either through his newspaper
or his "mummy" letters, did not diminish Page's interest
in North Carolina or the rest of the South.

The problem with the entire South was not so much
an inability to accept the "New South" industrial concepts, or an overweening attachment to the lost Confederate cause. Page's inability to effect change in these
areas stemmed from his insistence on rational discussion
of the Negro problem at a time when the emotional content of this question was rising sharply.[36]

North Carolina, for instance, made great strides
in upgrading its education system. The man responsible
for this was Charles B. Aycock, who was known as North
Carolina's "educational Governor."[37] However, in order
to get local tax approval for the new educational system, the Negro had to be shut out. The whole educational reform program of 1900 was tied to disfranchisement of the Negro, and could not be separated from it.[38]

Even Page, despite his hard efforts for Southern
education in general, acquiesced in the abandonment of
Negro education. Such motives can be found in the
activities of the Southern Education Board, which came
into being in 1901 to supersede the more religiously
oriented Conference for Education in the South.
"Heretofore its thought had been occupied chiefly with
Negro education; from now on its thought was occupied

with universal education, with adequate schools for the whites as the first thing to be provided."[39] The shift in emphasis is further seen in the stated purpose of the Southern Education Board. Within its organization, there was to be an "agency for the promotion of the industrial and general education of the colored people...to induce the white people to share in the active work, not only of aiding but of directing the development of colored schools."[40]

Furthermore, when Page was asked by a reporter to comment "if there was not a 'nigger in the woodpile'," he said: "you will find when the woodpile is turned over not a 'nigger', but an uneducated white boy. He is the fellow we are after. We want to train both the white boy and the black boy, but we must train the white boy first, because we cannot do anything for the Negro boy until his white friend is convinced of his responsibility to him."[41]

Page was here echoing the earlier comments of J.L.M. Curry, a colleague on the Southern Education Board and a leader in the push for Southern education. Curry stated: "We must proceed first to provide adequate opportunities for the whites. One properly educated white man will help to educate a dozen Negroes, while an illiterate white man will hold many more Negroes in the bondage of ignorance and degradation.... The education of the white youth of the South is the shortest road to the education of the Negro."[42]

Page's idealism, and his hopes for Negro education had been modified considerably by the time he became a member of the Southern Education Board in 1901. Indeed, his most positive editorial response in the pages of The World's Work, was a plea for silence on the subject of Negro domination which he felt continually interfered with the more important problems of educational advancement and industrial growth in the South.

Upon his return to New York, in late 1885, Page quickly converted his poverty into a semblance of comfort, writing on a free-lance basis in addition to his job as a leader-writer on the Brooklyn Union. He received $1800 a year, at that time a good salary, and shortly brought his family up from Raleigh, North Carolina. In addition, he ground out "political notes for the Nation and Harpers Weekly." It was during this period that Page became a member of the Reform Club, organized for promoting tariff reform after

Grover Cleveland's tariff message of 1887. Page's interest and ability, as well as his press position, soon led to the office of Vice-President and Chairman of the Reform Club's press committee. He was responsible for the creation and distribution of "plate matter," which was distributed all over the country. Apparently, "few private bodies have exercised such an influence on public affairs as the old Reform Club of New York." Page received no remuneration for his efforts, but he could boast that he had "millions of readers."[43]

For Page, however, the Reform Club provided a bonanza of associations and friendships which proved to be important in the future. Often, William Graham Sumner came down from New Haven for a meeting. Page also formed a friendship with Henry George. Here too, he met Henry Villard, Franklin K. Lane, William Gibbs McAdoo, and others who were, or soon would become, national leaders. The man whom Josephus Daniels had described as a poor mixer and politician had, by 1887, placed himself in a position of respect and authority among important men.

Page left the Brooklyn Union in February of 1887, and spent a few months on the New York Evening Post, then under the editorial guidance of E.L. Godkin. However, an opportunity to enter "that field of journalism to which Page had always regarded himself as predestined..." appeared. He was invited to join the staff of the Forum. The Forum was begun in 1885, by a group led by Mr. Isaac L. Rice. Originally edited by Lorettus S. Metcalf, a former editor of the North American Review, the magazine was in financial trouble by 1887. "Mr. Rice, a member of the Reform Club, became attracted by reports concerning Walter Page." Page joined the staff as business manager, but despite his efforts over the next three years, it continued to be a financial failure. Even efficient business management could not make up for the editor's inability to attract readers. Faced with suspension or reorganization, the owners chose Page "executive head of the whole enterprise." He became the owner of a substantial amount of stock, and a director.[44]

Like the most successful editor of Page's time, S.S. McClure, Page did not believe in waiting for material to come to him. Having an imaginary magazine in mind for each month, he solicited work from authors in hopes of achieving his ideal. Like McClure, Page never created the magazine he envisioned, a fact not at all surprising when one considers Page's high writing standards and the breadth of viewpoint from which he drew his articles. Page, too, "was no respecter of names or reputations; in considering the publication of literary material, he thought of nothing except its value at the time."[45]

This mania for timeliness often horrified the more literary editors such as William Dean Howells, who deplored the sensationalism and current events aspects of magazine literature.[46] Page, however, contended that "the magazine in the United States is the best instrument that has yet been invented or developed or discovered for affecting public opinion in our democracy. It gives the only way in which serious men can continuously reach the whole reading public."[47] Page firmly believed in public opinion, and obviously concerned himself with molding it. He sought to bring the public to share his own enthusiasms, yet, he maintained a high set of journalistic ethics. "That anyone should use the _Forum_ for personal ends seemed to him little less than treason to his readers." He neither took nor gave favors from interested groups or parties. Page had worked in the 1892 campaign for Grover Cleveland "both as chairman of the Press Committee of the Reform Club and as editor of the _Forum_. Despite the fact that the new administration "owed" Page some favors, he refused to solicit them, either for himself or for friends. He had supported Cleveland "because that seemed his duty as the editor of an honest periodical."[48]

> When Page took charge of the _Forum_
> its subscribers numbered about two
> thousand and its financial status was
> similarly languishing; by 1884 it
> had...a...circulation of twenty-
> eight thousand...No review in either
> America or Europe had ever acquired
> so many readers....the influence of the
> _Forum_ extended far beyond its group of
> immediate readers...newspaper...editors
> found in its pages material for the
> discussion of public questions, and its
> views constantly provided the 'keynote'
> for editorial judgements.[49]

Page's great success with the _Forum_, however, cannot be ascribed solely to his genius. In fact, an

13

entirely different story is recorded by Frank Luther Mott, author of the five volume History of American Magazines. Rather than a magazine on the brink of oblivion, Mott indicates that the Forum had been moderately successful, with a circulation of approximately twenty thousand by 1891.[50] Ostensibly, Page was hired as business manager to relieve Metcalf "from the burden of business management." While Page's efforts in this regard helped the magazine, a clash between editor and business manager, the latter in Mott's opinion looking toward the editorship, led to the resignation of Metcalf in 1891.[51]

The Review of Reviews, whose editor Albert Shaw was later to work with Page on various education boards, said of the Forum: "Many men in England have pronounced it the ablest and timeliest periodical of its class in the English language....[Page] may safely follow in the general line of policy which has in five years, brought the Forum to so commanding a position among periodical publications and to so strong a place as regards influence with the serious elements of the Community."[52]

Indeed, Arthur Bostwick has described Metcalf as having done previously most of the things which Hendrick ascribes to Page. "He had succeeded in assembling a notable group of contributors...gave them to understand that after he had accepted an article, it was his to do as he liked with." Metcalf insisted upon clarity especially because the Forum was used by schools and colleges.[53]

When Page took over, he was less meticulous with manuscripts. He retained the policy of enlisting "famous and expert writers to comment on significant affairs. Page also kept the second plank--the magazine-debate technique. Consequently, Page's editorship seems integral with Metcalf's, but it was more brilliant; and a greater stress on the distinguishing characteristics of the magazine, as well as a more acute sense of promotion and more insistence on timeliness, made a more attractive magazine."[54]

There is, of course, no doubt that Page made better use of the techniques he inherited than had his predecessor. Page was, according to both accounts, a tough editor. He could, and did, throw away articles already paid for when he thought they did not "get to the point" he had in mind. As editor of the Forum, in the spring of 1894, he threw out several articles on Grover

Cleveland which had been "obtained at great trouble and expense." In their place he substituted an unsigned article of his own, because not "one of them...has got the point."[55]

He especially insisted upon good straightforward writing. "He felt that no matter how important a man's message was, it failed if it were not written so that everybody would, and could read it." "Make it interesting was his uncompromising law....He used to say: 'Make your articles so simple and concrete that a Kansas farmer can understand them'....One phase of his genius lay in an almost uncanny ability to make what he wrote or edited so lucid that a child could grasp it. For so-called 'fine writing' he had an abhorrence. He believed in terse, direct, forceful Anglo-Saxon English ....Long articles were the bane of his life. He almost ranked dulness (sic) with murder."[56]

Page himself wrote clearly and directly, also "he was a master of letter-writing....Even his letters of rejection were treasured. O. Henry once said that 'a writer could take one of Walter Page's letters to a bank and borrow money on it.'"[57] Edwin Mims, professor of English literature at Vanderbilt University during the early years of the century, bears out this contention. In his opinion, Page "was a prolific letter-writer, undoubtedly one of the best of our time. In his very busy life he found time to write to a wide circle of friends and acquaintances. At a time when the stenographer is said to have destroyed the art of letter writing, the charm, and, I believe, the enduring literary quality of the masters of the craft."[58]

These fine qualities, which Page brought to the editorship of the Forum, no doubt helped its development into a financial success. However, the prestige of the Forum, prior to Page's leadership, was apparently quite great. The magazine was better established and more famous than Hendrick's account would indicate. Also, rather than sinking "into an obscurity from which it has never emerged,"[59] "the Forum's high point of circulation, double that reached under Page's management came 30 years later."[60]

An attempt to broaden the ownership base of the Forum eventually led to Page's departure from the magazine. Believing that a combination of business and editorial management was inadvisable unless "editorial policy could remain supreme," Page had been satisfied with the initial arrangement made in 1891. By 1894, he sought to attract new stockholders, men of literary interests, who might control the Forum through owner- ship and themselves contribute to its pages. However, because his original stockholders were all businessmen, "of foreign extraction...[of whom] only one or two possessed any education or had a speaking acquaintance with literature,"[61] Page's own conception of what the Forum could become was frustrated. "Every periodical," he wrote to Daniel Coit Gilman in 1894, "has some limitation to its public service--in most cases the limitation of ownership....The periodicals, therefore, yet but half serve the public. Now the Forum has a chance to be an exception....It is free. Nobody owns more than a small interest in it." The one thing needed, to make the Forum into a "great institution" was "the active cooperation through ownership of a large group of the most fertile and public-spirited men.... for if it had ideas enough...its circulation would be multiplied beyond all present expectations, and it would become a property of enormous value."[62]

When Page proposed, during 1894, to raise addi- tional capital by selling stock to outsiders, the original stockholders accepted. However, when it be- came clear that control of the potentially valuable Forum might actually fall to Page and his new stock- holders, the sale of new stock was stopped. This left "Page and his companions in the minority," and when Page was called upon to vote with the "commercial ele- ment" against his friends, he resigned in protest against what he regarded as a "dishonourable proposal."[63]

Page's personal financial arrangements, as editor of the Forum, had evidentally been satisfactory. His bid for full financial control stemmed from his desire to eliminate unnecessary business considerations from restricting literary excellence. As the magazine had begun to show profits in 1893, it was not surprising that Isaac Rice and his group should be reluctant to give up control of an investment which had just begun to pay off.[64] It was obviously easier to get a new driver than a new vehicle. Page's longstanding desire to be in control of his own periodical, beginning with his investment in The Age and continuing through his failure with the Raleigh State Chronicle, was again frustrated. He was, however, a valuable property in himself, and his resignation from the Forum in 1895 did not reflect adversely upon his ability. The kind of audience Page attracted as editor of the Forum, or at least, some of those who commented regretfully at his departure, included William Graham Sumner, Woodrow Wilson, Charles W. Eliot, Edward Atkinson and Jacob Riis.[65] He accepted a position with Houghton, Mifflin Company, as a literary advisor, and quickly moved into what at that time was "the premier editorial chair in the United States--that of the Atlantic Monthly."[66]

The Atlantic Monthly, of Boston, occupied, in the words of the Dial, "a place by itself...[and] stood more distinctly for culture than any other American magazine."[67] Its lack of contemporanity, despite its literary excellence, kept its circulation minute, approximately seven thousand in 1897.[68]

The editor of the Atlantic Monthly, when Page joined the magazine, was Horace E. Scudder, whose other duties with the Houghton, Mifflin and Company enterprises made the Atlantic "seem the least of his duties." His methodology differed from Page's more active and contemporaneous view. "...one thing I have never done," Scudder related to Ellery Sedgewick, "I have never invited a contribution to the Atlantic. If it is offered, I receive it. If it is good, I print it."[69] Despite this difference in editorial viewpoint, Page and Scudder became warm friends, and remained so after Page left the Atlantic.

An alternative view is offered by Bliss Perry, who succeeded Page as editor of the Atlantic. "...the attitude of Page's editorial co-workers," he wrote,

> "was one of restrained acceptance.
> Some were thrown off by his bluntness
> and informality, and basically they
> were skeptical of his editorial
> soundness. The severest of them was
> Scudder. Throughout the year that
> he was in Europe he wrote Page carp-
> ing criticisms of each successive
> number, and his well-meaning but
> tiresome meddling after he returned
> was no doubt irksome to Page. Scudder
> distrusted Page's judgement and
> considered him an iconoclast."[70]

Ellery Sedgewick, a later successor to the editorship of the Atlantic, began his journalistic career under Page. He reported that "no man ever gave me more valuable hints on editing than Mr. Page. Any boy would have been excited by his energy and courage. The self-confidence of his vigorous mind was a thing to wonder at."[71]

Another of Page's young assistants at the _Atlantic_, MacGregor Jenkins, saw him as a man of many moods and facets. Page "...became...a source of tremendous inspiration, displayed...kindness and consideration... [and] my brief contact with Walter Page taught me more about publishing than I had...learned before or have acquired since."[72] Indeed, Page worked closely with his associates, but it appears that he seldom gave up control of editorial policy.[73] Jenkins also reports that "the outstanding impression he made on me was that of intense intellectual restlessness...he impressed me ...as a man who had not found himself." Page was a master of the English language, both written and spoken, but he entered into the office dialogue with a rough and ready vernacular.

Despite wide variation of viewpoint, and differing relationships, most people who worked with Page seemed to like him personally. While Jenkins, Ellery Sedgewick and Isaac Marcosson all worked for Page, his partner, F.N. Doubleday, spoke as a peer. Doubleday refers to the "kindliness and optimism" of Page's editorials in _The World's Work_. Also, his magnificent letter writing ability, and the fact that Page "was ever courteous, quick, and interested" in "every person with whom he came in contact, if the new acquaintance was not absolutely and hopelessly dull."[74]

Where most spoke of Page as an exciting editor to serve, a pleasant and congenial companion, a slightly darkened view by the iconoclastic author of _The Jungle_, Upton Sinclair, upholds the basic outline. "He was," wrote Sinclair, "an extremely kindly and extremely naive gentleman; being good himself, he believed that other people were good."[75]

Actually, Horace Scudder was in delicate health, and although he remained titular head of the magazine, the major editorial activity fell to Page in 1896. While Page was able to enliven the _Atlantic_ somewhat prior to his assumption of full control, it appears that Scudder's influence was felt. "Literature is never more true than when it is serene," wrote Scudder to Page, in "gentle protest" over an issue full of controversial articles.[76] Page was still officially an

assistant editor when the Atlantic shocked Boston by
displaying unfurled the American flag on its cover, and
endorsing the annexation of the Philippines. Scudder
himself applauded this stand, and wrote from Europe
advocating an even more extreme policy. Thus by August
of 1898, when Scudder retired and Page officially became editor, the Atlantic's editorial policy firmly
bore the marks of his aggressive influence.

Besides the editorship, Page inherited Scudder's
duties as literary advisor to Houghton, Mifflin and
Company. Now 43 years old, these duties drained even
the robust Page. He continually complained that his
duties as book editor for Houghton, Mifflin and Company
precluded his doing a top job as magazine editor.[77]
However, Page had an excellent literary sense. He
brought to Houghton, Mifflin and Company the works of
Ellen Glasgow, and Mary Johnston, whose To Have and To
Hold is said to have doubled the Atlantic's small circulation while it ran serially.[78] He also had occasional failures. The most notable of these was his
rejection of Edward Wescott's David Harum, partly on
the advice of a literary assistant. The book, prior
to being offered to Houghton, Mifflin and Company, had
been rejected by several other publishing houses. It
made a fortune for its eventual publisher.

Page's position with Houghton, Mifflin and Company,
as both editor of the Atlantic Monthly and chief
literary advisor, was the first, but not the last time
he would fulfill both roles. This experience, while
exhausting, rounded out his education as an editor.

FOOTNOTES
CHAPTER I

[1]Josephus Daniels, <u>Tar Heel Editor</u>, (Chapel Hill, N.C., 1931), pp. 437-38.

[2]Burton J. Hendrick, <u>The Training of an American</u> (Boston, 1928), p. 12. All other information on Walter Hines Page's childhood and early life for which no citation appears may be presumed to be from this source. Quotations from this source will be cited hereafter as Hendrick, <u>Training</u>.

[3]Daniels, p. 437.

[4]Hendrick, <u>Training</u>, pp. 23, 27.

[5]Hendrick, <u>Training</u>, pp. 49-50.

[6]Hendrick, <u>Training</u>, pp. 56-57.

[7]Hendrick, <u>Training</u>, p. 29.

[8]Hendrick, <u>Training</u>, p. 63.

[9]Hendrick, <u>Training</u>, pp. 63-65. This love long preceded the effects of "subtle flattery" during Page's ambassadorial days. Page's love of England, says Hendrick, "...was no improvised conviction." Yet Hendrick denies that Price, who acknowledged no greatness in Northern writers like Hawthorne, Emerson, Longfellow or Whittier, affected Page in his admiration for these men. Nor, did Page suffer a loss of his personal sense of American nationalism, despite Price's feeling that "...Virginia was his 'native country', and England his 'mother land.'" (<u>Training</u>, p. 66.) Hendrick's selectivity of influences here is too clear cut to be totally believable, but Page's own future history gives credence at least to a love of literature and a dedication to good writing.

[10]Page to his cousin, Sara Jasper, Sept. 30, 1876 and Oct. 15, 1876. Cited in Hendrick, <u>Training</u>, pp. 75-78.

[11]Page to Sarah Jasper, Nov. 30, 1876, cited in Hendrick, <u>Training</u>, p. 77.

[12]Hendrick, *Training* p. 92 _ff_. Hendrick's considered opinion is that Page did not at this time develop a dislike for either the country or the people, and "in the main, his attitude was sympathetic."

[13]Hendrick, *Training*, pp. 105-106. Undated letter.

[14]Hendrick, *Training*, p. 109.

[15]Hendrick, *Training*, p. 121.

[16]Hendrick, *Training*, pp. 121, 123.

[17]Hendrick, *Training*, p. 126.

[18]Hendrick, *Training*, p. 130.

[19]Hendrick, *Training*, pp. 130-131.

[20]Page's comment, quoted in Hendrick, *Training*, pp. 133-134.

[21]Hendrick, *Training*, p. 157.

[22]Hendrick, *Training*, p. 159.

[23]Hendrick, *Training*, pp. 160-162.

[24]Hendrick, *Training*, pp. 164, 166-167, 168.

[25]Charles William Dabney, *Universal Education in The South* (North Carolina, 1936), II, 182.

[26]Hendrick, *Training*, p. 171. See also Charles William Dabney, *Universal Education in The South* (North Carolina, 1936), II, 184-185.

[27]Dabney, *Universal Education...*, II, 185.

[28]Dabney, *Universal Education...*, II, 182-189. Dabney was himself one of the original members of the Watauga Club. His account of Page's activities is less partisan than Hendrick's.

[29]Hendrick, *Training*, p. 173.

[30]Josephus Daniels, *Tar Heel Editor* (Chapel Hill, N.C. 1939), pp. 96-97.

[31]*Ibid*., p. 256.

[32]Charles Grier Sellers, "Walter Hines Page and the Spirit of the New South," The North Carolina Historical Review, XXIX, Oct. 1952, 486-487.

[33]Robert D.W. Connor, "Walter Hines Page," Southern Pioneers in Social Interpretation, ed., Howard W. Odum (Chapel Hill, N.C., 1925), p. 55.

[34]Burton J. Hendrick, The Life and Letters of Walter Hines Page (New York, 1923), I, 45.

[35]Robert D.W. Connor, "Walter Hines Page," Southern Pioneers in Social Interpretation, ed., Howard W. Odum (Chapel Hill, N.C., 1925), p. 55 ff.

[36]Ibid.

[37]Hendrick, Training, p. 191.

[38]Louis B. Harlan, Separate and Unequal: Public School Campaigns and Racism in the Southern Seaboard States 1901-1915 (Chapel Hill, N.C., 1958), pp. 75-101, especially, pp. 95 ff.

[39]Dabney, Universal Education..., II, 39.

[40]Ibid., p. 58.

[41]Ibid., pp. 45-46.

[42]The Winston-Salem Daily Sentinel, April 19, 1901, in Dabney, Universal Education..., II, 39.

[43]Hendrick, Training, pp. 195-196, 198-199.

[44]Hendrick, Training, pp. 202-203.

[45]Hendrick, Training, p. 216.

[46]William Dean Howells, Life and Letters (New York, 1902), p. 11, in Frank Luther Mott, A History of American Magazines (Cambridge, Mass., 1957), IV, 36.

[47]Hendrick, Training, p. 205.

[48]Hendrick, Training, p. 217.

[49]Hendrick, Training, p. 227.

[50]This is ten times the circulation attributed to

the Forum by Burton Hendrick.

[51]Arthur E. Bostwick, A Life with Men and Books, pp. 125-126, cited in Frank Luther Mott, A History of American Magazines (Cambridge, Mass., 1957), IV, 514. Bostwick's position as an assistant editor on the Forum was lost in the editorial changeover, a fact which raises some question of his objectivity as a source.

[52]Review of Reviews, April, 1981, p. 288.

[53]Arthur E. Bostwick, A Life with Men and Books, p. 126 cited in Frank Luther Mott, A History of American Magazines (Cambridge, Mass., 1957), IV, 515.

[54]Mott, IV, p. 515.

[55]Mott, IV, p. 516. See also Burton J. Hendrick, The Life and Letters of Walter Hines Page (New York, 1923), I, 51-52.

[56]Isaac F. Marcosson, Adventures in Interviewing (New York, 1919), pp. 40-41.

[57]Ibid., p. 41.

[58]Edwin Mims, "Walter Hines Page: Friend of the South," The South Atlantic Quarterly, XVIII (April, 1919), 101.

[59]Hendrick, Life and Letters..., I, 53.

[60]Mott, IV, 515n.

[61]Hendrick, Training, p. 228.

[62]Hendrick, Training, pp. 230-231.

[63]Hendrick, Training, p. 232.

[64]Journalist, IX (Dec. 16, 1893) 2; Cited by Mott, IV, 516.

[65]Fredrick B. Weaver, "Walter Hines Page and the Progressive Mood," unpublished doctoral dissertation (University of North Carolina, Chapel Hill), pp. 105-106.

[66]Hendrick, Training, p. 232.

[67] *Dial* (Oct. 1, 1902), cited by Mott, IV, 44.

[68] Mott, IV, 44.

[69] Ellery Sedgewick, *The Happy Profession* (Boston, 1946), p. 155.

[70] Bliss Perry, *And Gladly Teach: Reminiscences* (Boston, 1935), p. 165.

[71] Sedgewick, p. 155.

[72] Personal communication to Burton J. Hendrick, *Training*, p. 274.

[73] Sedgewick, p. 155. See also MacGregor Jenkins view in *Training*, pp. 274-275; George Doran, *Chronicles of Barabbas* (New York, 1935), p. 42; and of course, Upton Sinclair, *The Autobiography of Upton Sinclair* (New York, 1962) p. 163 on this point.

[74] Frank Nelson Doubleday, Introduction to the 1923 edition of Walter Hines Page, *A Publisher's Confession* (New York) pp. x-xii.

[75] Upton Sinclair, *The Autobiography of Upton Sinclair* (New York, 1962), p. 163.

[76] Hendrick, *Training*, p. 273.

[77] Page to Horace Scudder, May 5, 1899, Page MSS, Harvard University. Quoted by Fredrick B. Weaver, "Walter Hines Page and the Progressive Mood," unpublished doctoral dissertation (University of North Carolina, Chapel Hill, 1956), p. 124.

[78] Frank Luther Mott, *A History of American Magazines* (Cambridge, Mass., 1938) II, 512.

CHAPTER II

THE FORMATION OF DOUBLEDAY, PAGE & COMPANY
AND THE WORLD'S WORK

Despite the prestige which the editorship of the
Atlantic brought to Page, it was not as remunerative
as he would have liked. Thus, when Samuel S. McClure
began in June of 1899 to besiege Page with telegrams,
inviting his services for McClure's expanding publishing empire, Page found these overtures hard to resist. [1]
McClure and Frank Nelson Doubleday, along with John
Phillips of the McClure organization, had entered into
an agreement with J. P. Morgan to rescue the house of
Harper. In order to do this, and still operate his
magazine and book publishing business properly,
McClure needed additional talent. He enticed John
Finley, then President of Knox College, to join the
enterprise as editor of Harper's Weekly. [2] Page came in
as editor of the Harper and Brothers book publishing
department, Doubleday remained at the head of McClure
and Doubleday Book Publishing Company, John Phillips
had overall control of Harper & Brothers, and Ida
Tarbell became editor of McClure's Magazine. [3]

For Page, McClure's offer was financially irre-
sistable. "Page was to be editor of the encyclopedia.
For this he would be paid fifteen thousand dollars a
year, plus fifty thousand dollars in stocks and royal-
ties worth, McClure's words, 'untold thousands.'" [4]
Page was almost embarrassed to take a job for money,
but he also despaired of achieving his goals, as editor
of the Atlantic, in leading an "intellectual and not a
clerical life." [5] The editorship of McClure's encyclopedia was accepted, partly for the money, and partly
in the mistaken idea that other editorial possibilities,
more akin to Page's talents would become available
through the acquisition of Harper & Brothers by
McClure. [6]

With the new opportunity had come greater freedom
and less pressure. Writing to his friend Horace
Scudder, in November of 1899, Page indicated how much
he enjoyed going out to find material. He was free
"...from having to read millions of poems and stories
and to make up magazine schedules....was quite happy
...when I came home from ten days' absence...with the
promise of thirteen books for the next spring and fall

lists. That's fun compared with office work....its
hard to get weaned from Cambridge and 4 Park Street--
hard till I recall that 4 Park Street meant eight hours'
office work a day and the consequent rheumatism of knee
and brain..."[7]

The new freedom, however, was short lived.
McClure had overreached himself financially and his
business relations with Frank N. Doubleday were deteri-
orating. Doubleday himself did not care to play
second-fiddle to anyone, and his relationship with
McClure, Phillips and the whole McClure's organization
had been difficult from the beginning. Doubleday, in
fact, was a businessman first and an editor second,
making his publishing orientation exactly opposite
that of McClure. George Doran, in his reminiscences,
stated:

> Doubleday I had known as a book lover
> --singular--with a complete fidelity
> to one red Russia leather-bound book,
> the book of law and the profits....
> Long since I had learned that in the
> Doubleday economics of publishing
> the auditor-in-chief and not the
> editor-in-chief was the final arbiter
> of publishing policy.[8]

In order to save his floundering empire, McClure
proposed a financial reorganization. Doubleday, however, would have been only a junior partner in this
new scheme, and refused to go along. Consequently,
the agreement to purchase Harper & Brothers had to be
vacated by McClure and his associates.[9]

The break between McClure and Doubleday came two
weeks after the Harper purchase had been vacated.
Doubleday dissolved the partnership and took Page with
him.[10] The dissolution of the Doubleday & McClure
Book Publishing Company was not immediately finalized,
although Doubleday began the process of severing his
connection with McClure within a few weeks of the
Harper & Brothers forfeit. With Page, Doubleday formed
a new company, Doubleday, Page & Company, recruiting
Samuel A. Everitt and Henry W. Lanier as additional
partners.[11]

The new company, which officially formed in
February 1900, was a going concern from the beginning.
Doubleday brought with him the most important author of

the Doubleday & McClure Book Publishing Company,
Rudyard Kipling, who was also a close friend of
Doubleday.[12]

For Doubleday, little actually changed. He pro-
ceeded to run two companies simultaneously, Doubleday
& McClure Co. and Doubleday, Page & Company. The
former soon became only a paper company, as everyone's
efforts went into the Doubleday, Page & Company book
lists. During the early months of 1900, McClure was
not supplanted, he was circumvented by the devices of
keeping the old company legally alive.

"We have had our interview with the lawyer," wrote
Doubleday, "and find that there is absolutely nothing
to prevent our forming a new company or partnership,
except that we must take care of the old and keep it in
good shape. As long as Doubleday & McClure Company
pays its debts and is properly conducted, there is no
possibility of our being interfered with in any way,
and of course, we expect to do what is right by the old
company as we do by the new." McClure, in the depth of
financial difficulties and personal defections, was in
no position to challenge Doubleday's actions.[13]

In late February, 1900, Doubleday wrote to Page in
Chicago, where he was speaking; "How do you like the
looks of this note-paper? We are having our stationery
prepared so we can start in at once to use the new firm
paper when we wish to." The new Doubleday, Page & Co.
letterhead carried the same address as the old Doubleday & McClure Co. had, and Doubleday was, indeed,
continuing to publish his, and McClure's old list while
sending Henry W. Lanier and Walter Page after new
authors. Doubleday bided his time, letting McClure's
interest slowly lapse.[14]

The new organization soon offered Page the opportunity to edit his own periodical. This was the ful-
fillment of a personal dream which began with The Age
in Louisville, Kentucky, and was frustrated when he
clashed with the ownership of the Forum over financial
control. Once the initial period of development and
consolidation had passed, Page's efforts during the
second half of 1900 were bent toward the creation of a
new magazine.

Eschewing the non-editorial policy of the Forum,
and continuing the widened conception which he brought
to the Atlantic, Page sought to create a magazine which

would "represent the new impulse in American life--the new nationality--and...would do so with energy, aggressiveness, and, if...necessary...with unmannerliness."[15]

This protestation to William Roscoe Thayer brought a response in which Thayer professed to be disappointed in the non-literary attitude of The World's Work. He admitted that it certainly would be useful to the public, but "what opening does it afford for the best work?"[16] Page, who was successful on the Atlantic despite his supposed lack of a "literary soul," declared a year later that his purpose was to present the "literature of achievement...the literature of action." Furthermore, Page asserted that "work on a magazine had little to do with literature. Rather, it was journalism." His magazine was not to be a showcase for the publishing house, but an entity in itself.[17] Literary advertising would be just that, as distinct from the other features of the magazine as life insurance or soap advertising.

The magazine's title, The World's Work, came from Rudyard Kipling. During a conference on the magazine's future title, Kipling stated, "What you really want is a magazine that deals with the work of the world." "There it is," Page exclaimed: The World's Work." Page completed the title, making it The World's Work: A History of Our Times.[18]

Within the limits of possibility, Page had full charge of the magazine.[19] However, business and editorial activities were always closely integrated, especially as the magazine was not designed to be written off as advertising.[20]

Apparently, the magazine flourished almost from the beginning. Page reported, at the end of the first six months, that the magazine "immediately established itself, and has won a larger patronage...than any other periodical of high aim has won during a similar period, under modern publishing conditions." This, he stated, proved the soundness of "interpreting the important achievements of contemporaneous life...".[21]

Page reiterated this theme of the success of his editorial conception at the year's end. This issue, October, 1901, carried 102 pages of advertising, partially literary, only 13 of which were Doubleday, Page and Company advertising. Twenty pages were devoted to advertising the Booklover's Library, which advertised correspondent courses and subscription sales. Discounting these both, there were still 69 pages of paid advertising, against 116 pages of text.[22]

On the second anniversary of The World's Work, Page reported that the magazine had been placed originally upon a trial basis. "If it did not prove itself quickly, it should be abandoned....If it had to be kept alive by the sheer force of money, it were not worth keeping alive." But, the conception upon which the magazine was based, the excitement of American industry and commercial activity, attracted support from those same elements, making promotion of American commerce into a paying proposition. Indeed, "the little sum of money that the magazine was born with was not needed for its rearing; for it quickly made its own way." Despite the fact that costs exceeded estimates, so too, did advertising revenue, or else, said Page, "this page would never have been printed to tell this story."[23]

In the October, 1903 issue of The World's Work, Page commented upon the soon to be occupied offices at 133-137 East Sixteenth Street.[24] The World's Work, he suggested, "has now become an institution. It has long passed the status of a mere personal enterprise. The public has accepted it...it is the public's...and those who have the privilege of conducting it so regard it." Page felt that the operation of an independent journal was a public trust. "Merely to write the truth, as one sees it, requires only a negative courage. But truthfully to interpret American activity and aspiration in their manifold forms requires the courage of openmindedness, as well as the art of knowing the right places for emphasis. If it is a useful achievement to have established such an institution, it is an even higher duty rightly to develop and guide it."[25]

It is presently difficult to gauge with accuracy the extent of The World's Work's financial growth during its first ten years. The growth of Doubleday, Page & Company, however, does not seem to be in doubt. The expansion which forced the firm to move from their original offices in 1904 into a building at 133 East 16th Street is prima facie evidence. This new building was built to specification for Doubleday, Page & Company. In 1907, the firm was forced to abandon the less than two year old Farming Magazine, which had not carried its own weight. It was consolidated with the successful Garden Magazine, which was thereafter known

as The Garden Magazine and Farming. Despite this
failure, Doubleday, Page & Company was paying a divi-
dend of 1% per month in 1907.[26]

By the end of 1910, the new building was obsolete.
Doubleday, Page & Company had purchased their own
printing equipment. Also, the 1908 purchase by Doubleday, Page & Company of the remains of McClure's publishing company had required an increase in personnel.
Doubleday, Page & Company paid $118,750 for McClure's
publishing company, a property already appraised low at
$225,000. This included a book list of over 1000
titles, and contracts with such authors as Joseph Con-
rad, O. Henry, Booth Tarkington, Willa Cather, Conan
Doyle and Jack London.[27]

"We have," wrote Doubleday to Page in June of 1909,
"about all we can digest." The problem, he suggested,
was not having too few books, but too many to properly
promote.[28] The overcrowding led to consideration of
yet another building, and improved transportation made
a move to Garden City, Long Island, desirable.[29]

The Doubleday, Page & Company magazines, with the
exception of Farming, were financially successful. So
indeed was the parent company. In 1910, the gross
profit of Doubleday, Page & Company was approximately
$215,000. For the 1911-1912 fiscal year, the estimated
gross profit was approximately $330,000. The World's
Work contributed about $35,000 during 1910, and $40,000
during 1911-1912.[30] The gross income from Country Life
in America was listed as $58,000 in 1910.

The circulation of The World's Work, in 1910, was
estimated at 126,500 by N.W. Ayer & Son's American Newspaper Annual and Directory. The previous year's figure,
submitted by the publisher, was 104,000. The publishers, in 1911, reported a circulation of 119,135.[31]
Country Life in America had a circulation of only
35,000 in 1910, but was published semi-monthly. After
1905, its subscription price was $4.00, one dollar
above the subscription price of The World's Work. This
helped to offset the increased cost of publication.[32]

For Page, the move to Garden City was financial
gain and physical loss. Three months of commuting from
their New York City home to Garden City led to a decision in late January, 1911, to move into quarters in
Garden City. By the end of February, suitable quarters
had been found, and a five year lease taken on a house

on Cathedral Avenue. By mid-April, the move was completed.[33]

Before he left Doubleday, Page & Company to assume the duties of ambassador, Page had achieved a decent level of financial comfort. He noted his holdings in Doubleday, Page & Company, in 1911, as 250 shares. Some financial reorganization evidentally took place between 1911 and 1912, as Page listed his holdings in 1912 as 950 shares of Doubleday, Page & Company common stock and 77 shares of Doubleday, Page & Company preferred stock. These paid respectively, $688.00 and $792.00 in both June and August of 1912. This, of course, was in addition to his regular salary as editor of The World's Work.[34]

It is safe to assume that the financial solidarity of Doubleday, Page & Company, by 1912, was unimpeachable. This left Page time and freedom to pursue his pet projects, Southern education and the election of Woodrow Wilson, although as editor of The World's Work he was heavily committed to his literary duties.

Walter Page's second son, Arthur, joined the magazine in 1905, and by 1908 begged to be allowed to take over some of the details which he believed kept his father from greater activity in the educational and book world.[35] In 1911, Arthur Page became the managing editor of The World's Work, but his management did not reduce the large demands on Walter Page's time.[36]

To some extent, these demands upon Page's time and attention were self imposed. Even before undertaking the editorship of The World's Work, Page had been actively involved in non-literary projects. The most important of these was Southern educational uplift. In a letter to Dr. Wallace Buttrick of the General Education Board, Page outlined a number of speeches he planned to give, mentioned articles soon to be printed by the Outlook and the Atlantic Monthly, announced the private publication of "The Rebuilding of Old Commonwealths" and requested suggestions for "editorials and articles along the same lines."[37]

At the same time, his additional literary duties for Doubleday, Page & Company were almost staggering. Everybody's Magazine was being edited and published in the Doubleday, Page & Company offices. Even before the inception of The World's Work in November, 1900, Page was advising Frank Leslie's Magazine. Doubleday,

Page & Company had also undertaken the American publication of the new <u>Monthly Review</u> of London.

These magazines had, for the most part, a literary rather than a current issue orientation, and thus did not present a conflict of interest. They were eager to "capitalize on Walter H. Page's skill and prestige in the field..." Besides the income from these services, the firm gained additional book advertising in literary magazines not directly connected to Doubleday, Page & Co.[38]

Besides "skill and prestige," Walter Page had a knack for developing fair and intimate relationships with authors. "Every great publishing house," he wrote, "has been built on the strong friendships between writers and publishers. There is, in fact, no other sound basis to build on...". He noted that recent failures in the publishing field failed to observe this simple fact. The singular relationship between Frank N. Doubleday and Rudyard Kipling made the success of Doubleday, Page & Company a certainty from the beginning. Into this new partnership, Page brought some of his finds from Houghton, Mifflin Company, most notably Ellen Glasgow. Others, such as Joel Chandler Harris and Frank Norris came to Doubleday, Page & Company because of an honest and friendly relationship with Page. "In the building of these friendships, Page excelled."[39]

Most important, Page realized that publishing was neither a simple literary nor a simple business proposition, but a balance of both. Success depended upon the honesty of the author-publisher relationship. But, there was also the public to be considered. A publisher should serve the public by doing his part toward "improving the public taste, and...increasing the circulation...of the great masterpieces of literature."[40] These, of course, were hard to recognize, but truly great literature would separate itself from that which was "written for money and published for money."[41]

Walter Page stated this position on literature and the publishing business most clearly in an anonymously published little book entitled <u>A Publisher's Confession</u> which appeared in March, 1905. The book was a compilation of ten articles which earlier appeared unsigned in the <u>Boston Transcript</u>.[42] Evidently, there was some confusion as to its authorship, especially because it dealt so directly with the publishing business as to be slightly embarrassing. In December, 1905, an editorial appeared in The World's Work entitled "The Commercialization of Literature." In humorous fashion, while recounting the response to the "little book," Page set forth a clear distinction between commercial writing and literature.

"...is it not all a question of definition?" he wrote, "...is it not impossible for literature to become commercialized? For as soon as any writing, in the purpose of the author, is touched with the commercial spirit, for that very reason....it forfeits all claim to be regarded as literature....Literature is written chiefly because it gives joy to the writer and satisfies an impulse to do good work."[43]

Naturally, the publishing business required some commercialism for economic survival, but despite this fact, Page persisted in viewing the publishing business as a service to authors and to society. The ability to transcend the commercial side of the business through personal relationships and intellectual interplay with authors was what, in his opinion, distinguished publishers from mere printers.[44]

However, Page was always careful to distinguish between book publishing and magazine publishing. "Periodical writing," he noted, "was not literature in the proper sense of the word." Literature he conceived to be writing that was meant to endure, and therefore, the province of the book. The magazine was written for the period, and must be contemporaneous. The past, except as background for some current issue, must be divorced from the present "in the proper conduct of a periodical."[45]

Magazines also had to be of general interest, and well-written as well as interesting. "Many a fool," he once said, "mistakes an important article for an interesting one....Magazine writing must do more than instruct; it must charm." An editor, in Page's opinion, was "...the man who gave vital direction to every page....His ideas, his 'personality,' must be felt; he must have a 'policy' of his own; his magazine, that is, must represent his own enthusiasms, his own interests." Finally, it must be national in scope. "A man who does not believe in this spirit, in democratic institutions, and in the eternal development of the character of the people under democratic institutions, ought to be hanged if he tries to edit a

magazine; because if that spirit be not in his work...
then his magazine is not worth having."[46]

Page remained true to this concept, throughout his
tenure as editor of The World's Work. He stressed
always the problems of the present, and did his best to
interpret them in a manner denoting his belief in progress and the continual uplift of American life. He
remained positive and constructive during a period in
which many other periodicals were seriously questioning
the basic values of Nineteenth Century America. And, he
remained hopeful that the best American values could be
salvaged from the whims of immoral men. In Page's view,
the discrepancies between theory and practice in
American life were due to the failures of men, not the
institutions through which they operated. The World's
Work, from 1900 through 1913, reflected this belief.

FOOTNOTES
CHAPTER II

[1]Burton J. Hendrick, The Training of an American (Boston, 1928), pp. 345-346. Hereafter cited as Hendrick, Training; Peter J. Lyon, Success Story: The Life and Times of S.S. McClure (New York, 1963), pp. 166-167. Hereafter cited as Lyon, McClure.

[2]Hendrick, Training, p. 348; Lyon, McClure, pp. 169-170.

[3]Lyon, McClure, pp. 169-170.

[4]Telegram, S.S. McClure to Walter H. Page, July 7, 1899, Page MSS, Harvard, quoted in Frederick B. Weaver, "Walter Hines Page and the Progressive Mood," unpublished doctoral dissertation, (University of North Carolina, Chapel Hill), p. 126. Hereafter cited as Weaver, Page.

[5]Walter Hines Page to Horace Scudder, August 2, 1899, quoted in Weaver, Page, p. 124.

[6]S.S. McClure to Walter Hines Page, July 7, 1899, quoted in Weaver, Page, p. 126. See also Lyon, McClure, p. 172.

[7]Walter Hines Page to Horace Scudder, November 4, 1899, quoted in Hendrick, Training, p. 350.

[8]George H. Doran, Chronicles of Barabbas (New York, 1935), p. 46. Frank N. Doubleday's "business is business" attitude is well described by Peter Lyon in Success Story: The Life and Times of S.S. McClure. Lyon's account of Doubleday's overweening desire to dominate in business is verified by Doran's memoirs, p. 223.

[9]Lyon, McClure, pp. 170-171. Hendrick's account of the "experiment", found on pp. 351-352 of Training, makes it appear that the cancellation of the purchase agreement was voluntary. Lyon, however, has the more complete account, and indicates that McClure would have held on had he been able to refinance his empire. See Lyon, McClure, pp. 159-173.

[10]Lyon, McClure, p. 172. Lyon quotes McClure as

35

stating that the loss of Page "hurt badly" for personal reasons. McClure had "not set much store by Page's editorial talents: in fact, he had planned only to put Page in charge of the projected encyclopedia." But because McClure needed to feel that everyone liked him, he told Doubleday that what really hurt was that Page "sort of preferred you to me."

[11] Hendrick, Training, p. 352.

[12] Undated memorandum, Page MSS, Harvard.

[13] Frank Nelson Doubleday to Walter Hines Page, February 24, 1900, Page MSS, Harvard. Written on Doubleday & McClure Co. stationery. See Note #9. According to Peter Lyon, McClure was in deep trouble financially after the failure of the Harper and Brothers purchase. Lyon imputes that Doubleday had not committed himself legally to back the Harper and Brothers purchase, and was thus in a position to retain his share of Doubleday & McClure Company without impairment. McClure, on the other hand, had committed everything he owned, and was struggling to hang on to his magazine and his syndicate. He thus had little time for the book publishing company, which had been operated-administrated by Doubleday while McClure pursued authors for his magazine and novels for the book publishing firm.

[14] Frank Nelson Doubleday to Walter Hines Page, February 26, 1900, Page MSS, Harvard. Written on Doubleday, Page & Co. stationery.

[15] Walter Hines Page to William Roscoe Thayer, December 5, 1900. Quoted in Weaver, Page, p. 185.

[16] Charles Downer Hazen, ed., The Letters of William Roscoe Thayer (Boston, 1926), p. 99, cited in Frank Luther Mott, The History of American Magazines (Cambridge, Mass., 1957), IV, 774-775.

[17] The World's Work, II (October, 1901), 1257.

[18] Isaac F. Marcosson, "Personal Portraits," The Bookman, XXXVIII (September, 1913), 22-25, cited in Weaver, p. 186.

[19] Isaac F. Marcosson, Adventures in Interviewing (New York, 1919), p. 42.

[20]Frank Luther Mott, The History of American Magazines (Cambridge, Mass., 1957), IV, 775.

[21]The World's Work, I (April, 1901), 584.

[22]The October, 1903 issue of The World's Work carried no more advertising than did the October 1901 issue, indicating that the magazine had size limits which were preset. As advertising charges in magazines are tied to circulation, the cost per page of advertising might easily have increased, even if the number of pages remained the same. Thus, the actual revenue in 1903 could have been in excess of the 1901 revenue. To be sure, the $3.00 subscription charge could not begin to cover the cost of publishing the magazine.
The circulation of The World's Work during its first five years, was estimated by N.W. Ayer & Son's Directory of Newspapers and Periodicals as follows: 1901 - between 12,500 and 17,000; 1902 - the same; 1903 - above 20,000, with the notation that "Advertisers value this paper more for the class and quality of its circulation than for the mere number of copies printed." Included in the Ayer & Son's Directory was a statement by The World's Work publishers to the effect that they printed "70,000 copies a month...to meet a demand that has been growing steadily." The Ayer & Son's Directory complained in a note in the 1906 issue that no satisfactory statement of circulation for either 1905 or 1906 had been received from the publishers of The World's Work, but continued to estimate their circulation as being in excess of 20,200. The 1907 figures were more explicit and more in line with the publisher's claims at 98,000.
By 1910, circulation was estimated at 104,000. 1911 and 1912 stabilized at just under 120,000. Prior to 1910, the circulation figures came from George P. Rowell's Directory of American Periodicals. This publication was absorbed by N.W. Ayers & Son's Directory of Newspapers and Periodicals in 1910.

[23]The World's Work, V (November, 1902), pp. 2695-96.

[24]Arthur Wilson Page, et al., The Country Life Press (Garden City, Long Island, 1920), pp. 7-10.

[25]The World's Work, VI (October, 1903), 3649. Page was perhaps somewhat presumptuous in his view that the public needed the important events of life interpreted for them. His diaries at the Harvard Library indicate his acceptance of the "stewardship" principle invoked

by Andrew Carnegie, at least to the extent that the best men should be in charge of the country and the economy. He harmonized this view with his belief in democracy by equating the "best" men with men of "proven worth." This outlook was very much akin to Thomas Jefferson's concept of an "aristocracy of merit."

[26]Page Diary, Harvard MSS, June 1, 1907.

[27]Lyon, McClure, p. 322.

[28]Frank Nelson Doubleday to Walter Hines Page, June 18, 1909, Page MSS, Harvard.

[29]See Arthur Wilson Page, et. al., The Country Life Press (Garden City, Long Island, 1920), pp. 7-13.

[30]Page Diary, Harvard MSS, February 27, 1911; March 20, 1911.

[31]N.W. Ayer & Son's Directory of Newspapers and Periodicals (Philadelphia), published annually.

[32]Frank Nelson Doubleday to Walter Hines Page, May 2, 1905, Page MSS, Harvard.

[33]Page Diary, January 22, 1911; February 28, 1911; April 17, 1911, Page MSS, Harvard.

[34]Datebook, 1912, Page MSS, Harvard.

[35]Arthur Wilson Page to Walter Hines Page, February 3, 1908; Page MSS, Harvard.

[36]Page Diary, January 22, 1911, Page MSS, Harvard.

[37]Charles G. Sellers, "Walter Hines Page and the Spirit of the New South," The North Carolina Historical Review, XXIX (October, 1952), p. 495; See also Hendrick, Training, pp. 407-408.

[38]Publisher's Weekly, November 3, 1900, p. 1234, quoted in Frank Luther Mott, A History of American Magazines (Cambridge, Mass., 1968), V, 73, 73n.

[39]Isaac F. Marcosson, Adventures in Interviewing (New York, 1920), p. 41; Hendrick, Training, p. 361.

[40]Hendrick, Training, pp. 354-355.

[41]Walter Hines Page, "The Commercialization of Literature," _The World's Work_, XI (December, 1905), 6926-27.

[42]_A Publisher's Confession_ was printed in 1905 by Doubleday, Page & Company, reprinted in 1907 by Houghton, Mifflin and Company, and twice more, in 1912 and 1923 by Doubleday, Page & Company. The 1923 edition contains an introduction by Frank Nelson Doubleday memoralizing his late partner.

[43]Walter Hines Page, "The Commercialization of Literature," _The World's Work_, XI (December, 1905), 6926-27.

[44]Hendrick, _Training_, p. 363; Walter Hines Page, _A Publisher's Confession_ (New York, 1905), p. 169.

[45]Walter Hines Page to Mark A. De Wolfe Howe, January 20, 1898, Page MSS, Harvard.

[46]Hendrick, _Training_, pp. 210, 206, 207.

CHAPTER III

THE POLICIES AND CONTENTS OF
THE WORLD'S WORK: 1900-1913

From the beginning, The World's Work was designed
to be a current affairs magazine. Virtually every possible topic, from agriculture to Zepplins might be
found in its pages. However, it was edited to reflect
the interests of Page, so that almost every issue
offered something on agriculture, banking, cities, education, health, government and politics, labor, immigration, railroads, safety, inventions, finance, and
commerce. The current affairs aspect of the magazine
came from offering the latest developments in each of
these subjects.

In the realm of politics and international affairs,
the magazine was truly a current events periodical.
Writing as close as possible to the publishing deadline,
Page utilized the editorial section to discuss the most
recent developments. As it happened, the magazine was
born at the end of the Spanish-American War, and its
first issues were dominated by the problems of ruling
the newly acquired overseas territories. Considerable
space was devoted to United States commercial relations
with Europe and Asia, and indeed, this was in great
part the magazine's reason for existing. The magazine's format and content, while generally consistent,
was occasionally changed radically to accommodate such
events as the Russo-Japanese War. The editorial policy
aimed at covering as many topics as possible in each
issue. Naturally, if any one subject was too comprehensive to be covered in one issue, a series of articles were run over a number of months. Such series,
however, were comparatively few prior to 1904, although
they came to comprise the majority of the articles
after 1908.

Editorially, Page stressed the positive rather
than the negative aspects of American life. He deplored sensationalism. Indeed, the word "cheerful"
appears in the vast majority of his editorial offerings.
He wrote, in July of 1905:

> Again, as hitherto at this time of
> the year, The World's Work presents
> a series of articles that chronicle

41

the advancement of the people in
other than material ways--the growth
of a popular appreciation of painting,
the making of pleasanter homes, the
beautification of our cities, the
building up of our schools for all
the people; for it is in these and
similar activities that our great
increase in wealth and prosperity
finds its justification. It is in
interpreting these things, too, that
a magazine which is given to the
explanation of our national development in its best directions finds its
highest usefulness. In these articles
there are no exciting contests over
the division of financial spoils nor
blood-curdling exposures of corporate
or political crime; but there are
hints of the higher life about which,
after all, we care more than for tales
of tooth and claw.[1]

Page declined to follow McClure's Magazine,
Munsey's, and the others into exposure for its own sake.
However, The World's Work pursued the "literature of
exposure" where it was commercially feasible to do so.

In 1903, the first such series was run. The subject was the corruption and inefficiency of the United
States Post Office.[2] In 1905 and 1906, The World's
Work attacked both the insurance and the meat packing
industries. The justification for such exposures was
that it was part of the public service aspect of the
magazine, indeed, its duty, to indulge in the literature of exposure when the arousing of the public mind
had a "constructive public purpose." A responsible
national magazine was obliged to step in when "the
natural channels of publicity were silent."[3]

It was the approach to social problems which made
The World's Work unique among magazines. Page's
"cheerfulness" and "optimism" translated his editorial
reportage of the insurance scandals of 1905-06 into an
issue which not only continued this exposure through
dispassionate reportage, but offered thirteen of the
seventeen articles in the April, 1906 issue to the
selection of life insurance, methods of escaping decep-
tion, the reorganization of the industry, and what kind
of insurance "men in the know" seek and hold. Page

often stated that criticism for its own sake was without value. Unless constructive reforms could be
offered, criticism was just carping. From its inception, The World's Work was filled with articles on how
to survive in the financial world. Thus, the special
insurance issue was an opportunity to educate on a
large scale by including both the problem and its solution in the same issue. The dispassionate approach to
both the insurance scandal and its solution was also
less offensive to important commercial interests.

Apparently, The World's Work lost its insurance
advertising anyway, having run a series of articles
exposing insurance abuses and industry corruption.[4]
Fortunately, a milk chocolate advertisement comfortably
filled the page formerly reserved for the Mutual Life
Insurance Company of New York, whose advertisement
appeared through the first two issues of life insurance
exposure before disappearing in January of 1906.

Another unique aspect of Page's editorial outlook
was his willingness to devote an entire issue to one
subject. Virtually every major exposition was covered
in its entirety. The August, 1904 issue was devoted
entirely to the Saint Louis Exposition. Apparently,
the demand for this special issue was great, as it was
bound separately by Doubleday, Page & Company. Other
such events covered by devoting a complete issue to them
were the "Wonderful Northwest" issue, describing the
Lewis and Clark Exposition at Portland, Oregon in 1907
and the Alaska-Yukon-Pacific Fair in Seattle, Washington in 1909. There were also issues devoted entirely
to vacations and vacation spots, and American overseas
trade, the latter entitled the "Looking Outward" issue.
Two of the most notable special issues were the Russo-
Japanese War issue in April, 1904, and the special
"Southern Number" of June, 1907.

In the case of the Russo-Japanese War issue, Page
had to scrap his previous plans and put his staff to
work on short notice to gather material in time for publication. However, since this war did not come as a
surprise, his staff was partially prepared for its
beginning. The World's Work had previously carried some
articles on the possibility of war, and Page had commented extensively in the editorial pages on the probable consequences of Russia's actions in Manchuria. For
most of the remainder of 1904, and into 1905, the war
received heavy coverage in The World's Work.[5]

The Special Southern number, in June, 1907, lauded the growth and development of industry and agriculture in the South. In Page's didactic manner, it also pointed out ways and means of further improvement. It is quite possible that Page tended to take a more positive view of man and society than was realistic, but his public display of optimism and cheerfulness, the qualities for which he is best known, did not preclude a certain private realism.[6] He admitted in a letter to Edwin Mims, that the South itself did not read his magazine in any great numbers. "...the Southern people don't buy magazines or books...I am therefore not at all surprised that we get no appreciable direct results. I have tried this sort of thing too often to expect much."[7]

Especially during its first years, and to a great extent throughout Page's tenure as editor, the main thrust of The World's Work was American commercial expansion. Of great interest was technology. Communications and transportation, seen by Page as being vital to the spread of Western technology, were set forth in articles on aircraft, balloons, shipping, tunnel building and the role of the automobile in commercial growth. Throughout these discussions, the men who built or created these wonders were lauded as the true geniuses of American society.

When viewed from an interpretive standpoint, the pronounced American nationalism of Page which led him to push American commercial supremacy in turn caused him to support white, actually English speaking, domination of the commercial world. Developments in transportation and communication would guarantee this supremacy. Finally, there was the near canonization of such figures as E.H. Harriman, John D. Rockefeller, Andrew Carnegie and James J. Hill, as being important business leaders whose character and perseverance were an example to all Americans.

Partly as the by-product of commercial nationalism, and partly in response to public interest, more articles which discuss the physical, cultural and intellectual inferiority of non-white nations appear in The World's Work after 1905. The September, 1907 issue contains both an article by Booker T. Washington, showing the uplift of the American Negro under white guidance, and an article on "The Mongolian as a Workingman" by Dr. Woods Hutchinson, which lauds the Japanese and Chinese worker on the West coast. In his

conclusion, Dr. Hutchinson generously states, "while
the Chinese and the Japanese have their defects and the
Coast has no desire to "gush" over them or urge them to
become citizens, we regard them as a valuable commercial
factor, and as a race free from vice or other drawbacks
as can reasonably be expected of mortals."[8]

Such articles as these were solicited by Page,
who was more concerned with the lack of a labor force
on the West coast than with the racial deficiencies of
that labor force. Other articles in the same issue, on
the United States role in Puerto Rico are similarly un-
flattering. In all articles of this kind, the status
of the inhabitants of such areas, in relation to the
Anglo-Saxons, was thought to be inferior.

In election years, Page devoted much of his editorial space to the candidates and questions at hand.
Nineteen-hundred and four had been a dull political
year, with an unknown Democrat seeking to oust Theodore
Roosevelt. The Russo-Japanese War had taken up the
slack nicely. In the absence of such diversions, the
Fifteenth volume of The World's Work leaned heavily
upon the forthcoming Presidential nominations and
election. A five part series on W.H. Taft was concluded in November of 1907, and December found Page
again, in his Christmas issue, thankful for such far
seeing men as J.P. Morgan, whose timely action had
helped to soften the effects of the financial panic in
1907. An article on J.P. Morgan began in January of
1908, as did comment upon the coming presidential
election year. Page was a free-trade Democrat who
waited patiently for Grover Cleveland's reincarnation.
Consequently, the prospect of the candidacy of William
Jennings Bryan was extremely distasteful to Page. He
wrote, "...his (Bryan's) nomination, if it be made for
sheer lack of another man, will be equivalent to the
surrender of his party before the contest begins."[9]
The Republican candidate would be, in Page's opinion,
either Mr. Taft or Mr. Charles Evans Hughes, and the
former appeared to be Page's favorite.

Almost hopefully, yet portentious of things to
come, the same issue contained a highly complimentary
article about Woodrow Wilson, President of Princeton
University. The author wrote, "...he has so impressed
himself on men of intelligence in many walks of life
that he has been spoken of as the right man for political offices of the highest dignity--Governor, United
States Senator, and President."[10]

Except for occasional editorial comments lamenting the failure of the Democratic Party to advocate tariff reform as its major issue, The World's Work editorial pages were filled with Roosevelt, Taft and Hughes. While far more temperate than a truly Republican magazine, the amount of space spent discussing the public attitudes of the possible Republican candidates reflected Page's paradoxical position in being a Democrat and a friend of business at the same time.

However, in the hope of averting the inevitable nomination of Bryan, Page pushed other possible candidates. In April, an article on Governor John A. Johnson of Minnesota appeared, even though Page had admitted in a March editorial that the Johnson boom was dead.

This apparent anachronism was due to the exigencies of editorial planning, and were rare occurrences. Articles on such subjects as automobile development, shipbuilding or travel were relatively timeless, in the sense that a month's delay in publication was not critical. Political articles were not immune to time. Indeed, even the basic problem of filling a magazine with well written and interesting articles of a timeless nature led Page to plan, after October of 1905, more comprehensive series. This device had the positive effect of holding readers from month to month, and made editorial planning considerably simpler. The subjects which were vulnerable to instant obsolescence were handled in the editorial section, and written as closely as possible to publication date.

Election or not, the magazine continued to cover the same sorts of topics it always had. The second half of 1908 found The World's Work offering articles on artists and leading sculptors, photographic safaris into Africa, and the usual educational, agricultural and labor relations topics.

The basically uninteresting political campaign of 1908 led Page to seek more exciting material. He struck journalistic paydirt in securing "Some Random Reminiscences of Men and Events" by John D. Rockefeller. The announcement that these articles were to begin in October of 1908 came in conjunction with the announcement that C.M. Keys, The World's Work financial editor, would begin a series of articles on Standard Oil and its world-wide operations in August, 1908, in the special "Overseas Trade" issue. Page described

Rockefeller as "a remarkable personality" and was pleased that the public, which had "less authentic information...about any other notable man now alive," would have "a chance to see his great activities from his point of view, and with his large aims in mind."[11]

The point of view was certainly not to be one of exposure, as had been Ida Tarbell's articles in McClure's Magazine some years earlier.[12] Doubtless, the pro-commercial and generally laudatory attitude of Page toward important business leaders made the placing of Rockefeller's reminiscences in The World's Work a logical step. It indicated that the magazine had both safety and circulation.

In the second month of the Rockefeller reminiscences, the publication by the Hearst papers of collusive correspondence between John D. Archbold of Standard Oil and Senator Joseph B. Foraker of Ohio created a sensation. The response of Page to this revelation does little to justify Frank Luther Mott's belief that while "Page was a strong believer in the greatness and the essential honesty of American industry and industrialists...from time to time he attacked abuses of the system."[13] Rather, Page maintained that the evidence was circumstantial enough to warrant doubt, and that the only guilt attributable to either Foraker or Archbold was impropriety, the impropriety of actions which would incur the suspicion of the public. Despite the certain possibility that Foraker's career was over, Page was mere concerned with the lowering of the high "standards of conduct" which was incumbent upon every public official. The Standard Oil Company was chastised for not conducting its business openly. If it would, the results would be to the company's benefit. Page wrote:

> It would be a very important event in
> our commercial and political life if
> your rich and strong company could
> have the confidence and esteem of the
> American people, and if they pointed
> with pride to it at once as a great
> American commercial triumph and an
> organization that exemplified the
> highest ideals in all its activities
> as it does in some of them. Then its
> good influence both on our business
> and our political life would be over-
> whelming....You must work in the open,
> or continue to be suspected and hated.[14]

Considering the editorial space utilized for comments on the need for publication of corporation records, and Page's certain knowledge of prevailing business ethics, his editorial on the Foraker-Archbold debacle, and his "word" to Standard Oil, appear incredibly naive. That Page often presented a balance of viewpoints on controversial issues is basically true. However, Page's response to the Hearst disclosure was at best wishy-washy, something Page himself would have heartily condemned had he not been caught in the middle of an embarrassing situation.[16] The Rockefeller reminiscences ran from October, 1908 through April, 1909. December and January of the same years found Andrew Carnegie contributing two articles.

As might be expected, The World's Work reflected the public's interest in such "progressive" topics as conservation. Page came down on the side of Pinchot in the Ballenger-Pinchot controversy, but consistent with his views of American commercial development, he wanted the country's resources developed with the public's interest protected. Page was aware that the true frontier was closed, but stressed that there were still areas where a man could take advantage of opportunities on the land. There were also the frontiers of science and technology to be considered, and in publishing the latest information on technological inventions, Page usually speculated on the vast potential for commercial development that such things as the telephone and the automobile might have.

During 1908, Page's long standing interest in agriculture was reflected in expanded commentary on that subject. He served, during 1908, on President Theodore Roosevelt's Country Life Commission at the President's request. It was both an honor and a pleasure for Page to serve along with Henry Wallace, editor of Wallace's Farmer, Gifford Pinchot of the United States Forest Service, and Liberty H. Bailey, a professor at the New York State College of Agriculture and a former editor of the Doubleday, Page & Company magazine, Country Life in America.[17] His interest in agriculture, especially in scientific agriculture, predated the formation of The World's Work. Page had followed closely the work of Dr. Seaman Knapp, who first through private contributions, and later as part of the U.S. Department of Agriculture, had set up demonstration farms to show communities throughout the United States how to increase the quantity and quality of their crop production. In keeping with this interest, The World's Work presented an illustrated article in 1908 which described Dr. Knapp's special train, with which he toured the South, setting up model farms.[18]

In 1909, Page's interest returned to commercial expansion. In a series of articles, the world-wide problem of the black, yellow and brown races was discussed, with emphasis upon the threat of their back-wardness upon U.S. commercial growth abroad. Editori-ally, Page pursued education, the dangers of stock speculation, and the need for banking reform which became so apparent during the financial panic of 1907. Of especial interest, was the tariff policy of President Taft. Page was disappointed in the failure of Congress to rise above the domination of certain commercial interests. Taft's formula of making tariff duties equal to the difference between labor cost of manu-facturers here and abroad was acceptable to Page, who saw the alternative as a sweeping reduction of the tariff by an angry public in the near future, or even worse, the imposition of an income tax.[19]

In his editorial assaults upon entrenched privi-lege, Page was always careful to distinguish between the selfish despoiler and the empire builder. He had no quarrel with wealth, and indeed, saw this as sym-bolic of character and superior ability in men such as Carnegie and Rockefeller, whose wealth was acquired, in Page's opinion, in the process of building up American commercial power. He had faith in the superior judge-ment and ability of these great captains of industry. Proudly announcing, in 1909, a series of articles by James J. Hill, the builder of the Great Northern Rail-road, Page wrote, "Mr. Hill has become our foremost practical thinker and authority on most of the factors of our national progress."[20]

Furthermore, Page continued to consider that the superiority of American and Western European technology besides creating the highest form of political and economic life, produced as well the highest forms of art and literature. The World's Work, therefore, continued to feature articles on leading artists and sculptors.

As had become his habit, Page announced at the end of each volume, usually in the October number, what his readers could expect in the forthcoming six months. Besides Elihu Vedder, an artist of some note, The

49

<u>World's Work</u> readers could expect to find, in the last
months of 1909 and the spring of 1910, series by
Gifford Pinchot, Dr. Frederik Van Eeden, described as
"poet, novelist, dramatist...foremost literary man of
Holland," and Booker T. Washington.[21]

Broadly speaking, between the years of 1907 and
1910, <u>The World's Work</u> concerned itself internationally
with trade, but less with politics than in earlier
years. Perhaps this reflected Page's own interests, as
Southern education took up a great deal of his time.
The magazine itself was growing shorter, more series
were run, and the number of contributors decreased.[22]
The articles during this period tended to be longer
than during the earlier years of the magazine, and were
generally more copiously illustrated with photographs
and diagrams.

In a rare deviation from established practice, an
article, rather than an editorial, speculating upon the
prospect of Theodore Roosevelt's return to public life
appeared during June, 1910.[23] Although still concerned
with contemporaneous events, the magazine during 1910
responded less to news as such and concentrated more in
persistent discussion of limited topics. Article planning reflected this emphasis during 1909, and in the
editorial section in 1910 the narrowing of interest
becomes apparent. Page concentrated more on agricultural problems, education, banking reform and railroad
development. Such important events as the death of
Edward VII, while not ignored, received no such coverage
as had the death of Victoria in 1901. Rather, those
topics where gentle persuasion and general education
might have an effect were stressed. This change was,
at best, a shift in emphasis, as the magazine had
always pursued such topics in addition to world trade
and important technological developments. During the
year, the same topics were covered, but not all at
once as before. The pattern after 1907, and especially
in 1909 and 1910, was to explore major topics in depth
and then abandon them for a time. The August, 1910
issue is an example. Three articles, "The Crime of
'The Pork Barrel,'" "A Congressman's Letters," and
"Schedule I--The Cotton Tariff" were placed together
and cited by the editor as explicatory of "the waste-
ful and dishonest system" by which Congress "throws
away millions" for special favors to its members through
ill-conceived rivers and harbors bills.[24] It is impossible to tell whether this shift to in-depth coverage of
such topics was due to planning necessity, the nature

of the topic itself, or to the editorial opinion that such concentration more effectively made the didactic point intended. The only exterior evidence pointing to planning necessity was the steady disappearance, after 1906, of the shorter features which had characterized the magazine. The section entitled "Among the World's Workers," which constituted short staff written articles on American inventiveness and technology, became sporadic in its appearance, and disappeared altogether by 1910. Similarly, the book reviews and short articles on currently popular authors disappeared entirely. From the format of the magazine, one would never deduce that it was published by a book publishing house. Topically, the last months of 1910 found The World's Work indulging in some safe exposures, most notably the continuing pension frauds. Page did not oppose pensions for war veterans, but from the inception of The World's Work, he had commented almost bitterly on pension misuse. The railroads, never fully under attack, were discussed in terms of the effect that their rates had on commercial prosperity. A survey of the titles of the articles which appear in The World's Work during 1909 and 1910 gives the impression that Page had a truly "progressive" orientation. The content of these articles, however, is considerably more circumspect and conservative. The magazine, however, was continuing to prosper, and Doubleday, Page & Company moved into its new plant at Garden City, New York, during October, 1910.[25]

The issue for January, 1911, the Tenth Anniversary Issue, was a classic of its kind. It contained articles on population growth, investment growth, and industrial expansion from 1900-1910. In its pages were also found portions of Booker T. Washington's Chapters From My Experiences which had been running serially since October. Washington stated therein the progress of the Negro race in a fashion most amenable to Page. Of especial interest was Walter Page's story of The World's Work since its inception.

In this review, Page reiterated some of the comments he had made on earlier birthdays, and contradicted others. He explained that following the birth of Doubleday, Page & Company in January, 1900, efforts were made mostly in finding good books to publish. But, given past experience, "A possible magazine... naturally hovered in our thoughts, although during this first year it took no definite form. Then one morning it was casually remarked that it was time we were

getting it going. We all knew that such a duty lay
before us." No time was wasted, Page added, "discussing scope and character" or in making prospectuses.
"The magazine could be but one thing, and that thing
would reflect our temperaments, our points-of-view, our
philosophy of life."[26] Also, it must be sincere.

As it happened, wrote Page, overconfidence offset
lack of solid financing, but all agreed that the magazine would have to carry itself. Even if inclination
had existed for carrying on a losing venture, the new
firm of Doubleday, Page & Company had insufficient surplus to do so.

Printed at the Norwood Press near Boston, Mass.,
its first trial edition of 35,000 copies evidentally
found enough market to warrant its continuance. Page
understood that the new emphasis in magazine literature
was on the present, and "it was upon this idea--of
definitely reporting and interpreting the life of the
present--that The World's Work was established; and it
was because it had this definite idea and a clear
purpose that it succeeded and--was imitated throughout
the magazine world."[27] Cited as having been imitated
were the investment features, later expanded to cover
insurance, and the full page photographic portraits
which appeared from the first issue.

Page claimed that the magazine had, through its
articles on finance, caused the modification of certain
practices in leading financial houses. So too, The
World's Work's advertising had never been false or mis-
leading, and businesses whose practices were even mar-
ginally doubtful had been excluded from advertising
space. If true, such practice by The World's Work was
laudable, but most probably the pro-commercial attitude
of the magazine attracted more advertising than it
repelled, and allowed the selection of solid advertising without having to pander to companies whose
business practices were doubtful.

Page attributed the advertising honesty of The
World's Work to a close relationship between the business and editorial staff, and to the fact that the
magazine was indeed sincere in its public service
efforts. Most important, he wrote,

> The proper conduct of a magazine
> rests on a few large principles,
> which become reasonably clear after

ten years of experience. It must be
uncompromisingly given to the public welfare and to no private or
special or local or party interests
of any sort; it ought to be owned
by the men who conduct it, free of
all alliances and obligations; and
they ought to have no other calling
and no other interests; it cannot
be and ought not be endowed, for then
either the spur to active service
would be lacking or the "endowers"
would assert themselves in the same
way as lesser mortals, for some
narrowing effect.[28]

As near as can be determined, Page lived up to
his own specifications. There did appear, in December
of 1910, an article on a mechanical cotton harvester
which Page had backed financially. Also, his concern
for railroads, and especially his editorial condemnation of certain state legislatures for attempting to
pass restrictive rate laws, was less than impartial.
This interest may in part be attributed to the fact
that Page owned a portion of the family railroad, the
Aberdeen and Ashboro Railroad, which his father had
built and which his brothers operated. However, it is
quite possible that most of the positions taken by
Page on industrial matters and those who opposed commercial expansion would have been expressed as they
were anyway.[29]

To assure that a magazine be sincere, Page felt
that its ownership should be public knowledge. In an
industry as intimate as publishing, no secrets could
be kept for very long. In line with this belief, Page
again decried the "myths" that both Andrew Carnegie
and John D. Rockefeller had, at various times, backed
the magazine. Page had indeed, during his days as
editor of the Forum contacted Andrew Carnegie for a
$50,000 loan in order to purchase control. He was
politely refused then, and the likelihood is that
Carnegie never had any financial interest in The
World's Work. Similarly, in answer to the claim that
John D. Rockefeller had subsidized his own memoirs,
Page stated that the only money which passed between
The World's Work and Rockefeller was paid to Rocke-
feller as "literary earnings" by the publishers.[30]

During 1911 and 1912, the renewed chances for

53

Democratic political resurgence led Page to devote
much space in The World's Work to this topic. Most
notable, during the latter half of 1911, was the
number of articles and editorials on Woodrow Wilson.
In addition to the usual coverage of railroads, health
problems and financial topics, education received a
larger than usual amount of attention. Prize winning
essays from a contest which began during late 1910 on
"The School of Tomorrow" were run in each issue.[31]
The World's Work continued the inward turning trend of
the 1907-1910 period through 1912. Articles on world
trade and foreign countries were fewer in number and
more articles by fewer authors, partly because of long
running series, marked the style of The World's Work
during this period.

Basically, a real interest in the tenets of political Progressivism, especially in its immediate goals
of social purification, found emphasis in a series
entitled "The Awakening of the Cities" by Henry Oyen,
whose contributions on slums in the first half of 1911
had acknowledged that economic dislocations could
effect personal opportunity. Oyen's commentary, however, reflected Page's own dilemma in maintaining that
the psychological despair called "slum sickness" could
be overcome only by a provision of decent housing at
low prices. This would provide, for the unfortunates
whose financial position had deteriorated, an environment conducive to self respect. Oyen presumed two
things which might lead to recovery of financial status.
First, that the individual who had fallen from grace
have done so through no fault of his own. Secondly,
that he have the basic instincts of thrift, character
and moral righteousness which would allow him to
utilize a helping hand to find his way back to "middle
class" comfort and respectability. The entire emphasis
was upon the individual's efforts at recovery of lost
fortunes, and acknowledged as an unchangeable fact of
life that economic dislocations, while often responsible for economic instability, were inevitable.[32]

The interest in Progressivism was further reflected by a renewed attack on the Post Office and a long
look at business-like government expenditures, echoing
the program of the Progressive insurgents in Congress.

George Perkins, the J.P. Morgan partner who was
to finance Theodore Roosevelt's 1912 political come-
back, offered two articles, in June and July of 1911,
on business morals and personal responsibility in

business. Biographical sketches of Woodrow Wilson,
Robert La Follette and Judson Harmon of Ohio, stressing
their progressivism, also appeared in mid-1911. The
emphasis on politics in The World's Work had its justification in the belief by Page that at last some
changes could finally be made. He chided those afraid
of proper changes in an August, 1911 editorial and
pointed out that the Congressional Record was again
alive and interesting. [33] The explanation, he wrote,
"is that political life is again earnest." [34]

In his usual end-of-volume announcement in the
October, 1911 issue, Page surveyed some of the possible
Democratic candidates for the forthcoming Presidential
nomination. He announced the beginning of a series on
Woodrow Wilson, by William Bayard Hale, to run from
October, 1911 to March, 1912. Considering the lead
time required to create such a series, there can be
little doubt that Page had chosen Wilson as his candidate as early as the end of 1910. However, Page continued to discuss the candidates of both parties with
as much impartiality as could be expected by an editor
who definitely knew whom he wanted.

The forthcoming twenty-third volume of The World's
Work included articles on the South by Page's old
friend, Edwin Mims, Professor of English at the University of North Carolina. The public furor over the
threatened dismissal of Dr. Harvey W. Wiley, whose
efforts led to the Pure Food and Drug Act of 1906, was
also discussed. Included too was a real plum for Page,
the personal revelations of Henry White, former secretary of the United States Garment Workers Union of
America, which echoed Page's views of unions as immoral
in tactics and badly in need of responsible leadership.

The issue for October, 1911, had no fewer than six
series, either beginning or in progress, out of eleven
articles. The length of the text had returned to 117
pages, although these included a lengthened gallery of
14 pages photographic portraits. Along with a discussion of the fall book list and a preview of forthcoming
articles in Country Life in America, Page announced
that henceforth The World's Work would eschew the wire
staple for a sewn binding which would allow the magazine to remain flat when opened. A new style of type
was to be used, and in November, 1911, the pagination,
now running to 15010, was to begin anew for each volume
of six months. [35]

"The mechanical improvements," wrote Page, "are proper accompaniments to what we hope is a continuous improvement in the contents of the magazine--articles that are worthy of careful reading, and judgements that are sound and somewhat venturesome rather than somewhat dead. Any fool can stand still, as all stones must. A magazine must go forward or die."[36]

"Eleven years is rather a long time to wear one dress," wrote Page in October, 1911. But the change of type face and binding only marked the end, rather than the beginning of editorial changes which had been in progress since 1908. The Twenty-third volume of The World's Work, beginning in November of 1911, had shifted its emphasis almost solely to internal matters. To be sure, the unrest in Europe after 1910 could not be totally ignored. The special "Christmas-Peace" number in December, 1911 took up the question of world peace, but in a broad and general manner rather than in specific terms. There was, due to interest in the domestic political and economic scene, no longer room in The World's Work for provocative and incisive articles like "Will England and Germany fight," which appeared during 1908.

Emphasizing the inward looking aspect of the magazine was the inclusion of a new feature, "The March of the Cities," which followed up Henry Oyen's series on "The Awakening of the Cities." Herein, exemplary municipal achievements were cited "as encouragement to one of the most important movements of progress of this time."[37] This feature continued to appear each month from November, 1911 until Page relinquished active editorial duties for the ambassador's post in Great Britain. In reality, Page's editorial interest in the cities had been apparent from the inception of the magazine.

Actually, it was the growth of Progressive thought, especially the body of ideas which was later to be identified as Wilsonian progressivism, which led Page to emphasize the antithetical themes of city growth and agriculture. Almost from its first issue, The World's Work had carried articles on the cities. These varied, sometimes stressing the possibilities of beautification, and at other times lauding the building of skyscrapers and subways. Both editorials and articles pursued the idea that the city was a necessary evil, a necessity for the growth of commerce and industry and an evil in what its negative physical and

social aspects had done toward degrading the quality
of life. During 1906, Page had taken a position on
municipal ownership of utilities which was hardly
positive. He saw such "gas and water" socialism as
potentially dangerous to free enterprise but admitted
that in cases where private franchises had resulted in
gross corruption, municipal ownership might be considered as a last resort. By 1911, Page had changed his
position to a more positive appreciation of the municipal ownership of some utilities. The success of some
cities in administering utilities apparently convinced
Page that even during periods of dishonest government,
municipal ownership guaranteed fair rates and decent
service more often than occurred under the old private
franchise system. Page's initial opposition to municipal ownership, and his cautious approach to it in later
years may be attributed to his belief in the reign of
moral men as the only way of guaranteeing good government. He simply did not believe that any political
system, capitalism or modified socialism, could operate
successfully without this essential ingredient.   In
this regard, Page had been anti-Tammany from the
beginning of his editorship in 1900. The World's Work
was very outspoken in its attacks on Tammany, but such
commentary disappeared completely after 1905. This
sudden cessation of Page's heartfelt vehemence toward
Tammany may have occurred through local political
pressure because The World's Work was published in New
York City. However, it's equally possible that Page
decided that such attacks ran counter to the "positive"
editorial approach of The World's Work.

The second continuous theme, agriculture, received
perhaps more space than any other single subject in the
pages of The World's Work. Page's dedication to Southern progress took an agricultural approach as well as
an industrial approach. It is ironic that he found
himself at sword's point with Josephus Daniels, champion of the Southern agriculturist against the "New
South" industrialists. While Page was clearly identified with this latter group, and never eschewed the
role of industry and transportation in Southern uplift,
he was always of the belief that such improvements must
rest upon a strong base of agriculture. As late as
1909, in his semi-autobiographical novel, The Southerner, Page stressed this point.[38] The real issue
between Daniels and Page was not the importance of
agriculture, but the role of the Negro in Southern uplift. Whether in agriculture or industry, the huge
black working force of the South needed training. For

57

this cause, for nearly thirty years, Page railed without real effect against the old guard of the South.

However, it was the virtues of rural life which Page promoted from the beginning. The very first number of The World's Work carried an article entitled "Back to the Land", the story of a city man's experience in truck farming. Over the years, this theme was magnified. The other Doubleday, Page & Company magazines, Country Life in America and The Garden Magazine, were evidence of the continuing public interest in rural values and rural living. These magazines sought to help those who lived of necessity in or near the cities to take advantage of the healthful and soul enriching values of country life.

Page's own answer to slums, to the immigrant pools upon which city bosses fed, was the decentralization of these populations. Preferring to slow or halt immigration altogether, he still felt the necessity of putting immigrant populations of "peasant" background back on the soil. This would accomplish first, the resurgence of morality in city politics, secondly, utilize the best abilities of the immigrant population, and third, give greater opportunity for the assimilation of truly American values by foreign groups. Standing above these, and in reality their motive force, was Page's simple Jeffersonian belief in the inherent virtue of getting one's living from the soil.

In early 1911, Page wrote to Wallace Buttrick, his good friend on the General Education Board, asking whether Buttrick believed that a World's Work "readers service" feature on how, where, when and why to buy a farm might be successful. "I have made up my mind," he wrote, "to try an important experiment in The World's Work...about which I wish to trouble you for your opinion." Page pointed out the increasing scarcity of cheap land, the rapid increase in land values. "Now, taking this fact as a starting point, I wish to turn The World's Work very definitely into an experiment to induce people to go to...and stay on the land." Page proposed to publish short articles about the land, give story examples of success, and invite inquiries from readers such as those "it now invites...about investment." The program would, in Page's opinion, attract honest land advertising to The World's Work and be a real public service to the "thousands of readers...who would like information...but...don't know any trustworthy place to look for it."[39]

Page wrote Edwin Mims also, sounding him for an opinion, and indicated that while such a feature appealed to him personally, he was loath to start something which would not be of interest to the readers. Page, however, believed it worth a try, and in the November, 1911 issue of The World's Work, entitled the "Country Life" issue, he offered the magazine's services as "honest broker" for those interested in farm information.

"Does Anybody Really Want A Farm?" was the title of his opening statement. "Do people really wish to get on the land? Do those that have poor farms wish to get better ones? Do salaried men...whose careers are limited in town really wish to win the independence that the country offers? Is the trouble the lack of information about...ways and means of getting back to the soil?"

Page pointed out that the value of farm land had doubled in the previous ten years. He stated that the "old isolation of farm-life has passed in most sections of the country. Yet, there's no rush to the land. The town continues to outgrow the country."[40] Indeed, this was the trend Page hoped to reverse.

For many years, The World's Work had been working to reverse the trend toward urbanization even while it lauded city development. The extensive articles on health always counted upon clean air and healthful food. Methods of agriculture, as demonstrated by Dr. Seaman Knapp's efforts in the South, were fully publicized. New developments in seed, machinery and irrigation were featured. Even the 1910-1911 publication of prize winning articles on education stressed the physical health of students and their free involvement in nature as the primary path to true learning.[41] Most importantly, the values inherent in land ownership, independence, self-reliance, hard work, and a real stake in the country would assure democracy in politics.

The response was exciting for Page, and indicated that the interest in farms and farming was still high among those who lived or worked in cities. He received 186 letters by January, 1912. Page promised to answer every inquiry about farms that was received, and to offer articles "explaining the possibilities of the land without sentimentality and glamour, and explaining also many of the pitfalls that beset the new farmer and how to avoid them."[42]

Indeed, Page never claimed that farming was glamorous, but rather that it was hard work. He believed that hard work led to success and independence; that it was the basis of morality. One did his duty to society by providing opportunity. Success depended upon character, perseverance, intelligence and thrift, no matter what occupation was undertaken.

From November 1, 1911 to January 17, 1912, the Land Department of The World's Work answered 410 inquiries about farms and farm lands from correspondents in thirty states of the Union, Mexico, Panama, Holland, Peru, Canada, Hawaii and Puerto Rico.[43] If nothing else, such response points up the wide circulation of the magazine. Through The World's Work Land Department, Page was attempting to supply an organization which would operate to offset the trend toward urbanization. He noted in April of 1912 that cheap land was still available, and farming was more profitable than ever. "Yet the drift to the cities is not checked because country life, except in comparatively small areas, is still unorganized." This situation would change quickly when country life became as organized, and thus as attractive, as town life.[44]

Despite the greatly increased emphasis upon agriculture, The World's Work during 1912 became a showcase for progressive causes. Politically, 1912 was the first presidential election year since 1892 which held any real hopes for a low-tariff Democrat like Page. The diversity of candidates, and the complexities of their views made for exciting journalistic activity. In Page's opinion, the two best candidates were William H. Taft and Woodrow Wilson, and despite his private opinion Page was scrupulously fair to all the candidates, printing in May, 1912 the personal platforms of Wilson, Theodore Roosevelt, Taft and Governor Judson Harmon of Ohio.

In a letter to Ray Stannard Baker, Page commented on the many shades of Progressive political ideology. "God bless us," he wrote, "we now have Progressives, Halting-Progressives, Ultra-Progressives, Progressive-Conservatives, Conservative Progressives, and T.R.—the devil take the hindmost! T.R. is eternally right, too.*---* But Wilson's the man."[45]

The topical articles which appeared in The World's Work during 1912 were in reality only a concentration of ideas and interests which Page had pursued since

60

1900. He was excited about the prospect of a rejuvenated Democratic party, already showing itself in Congressional action, and sought to educate the public to ask for and support changes. Toward this end, the long standing attack on pensions was resurrected and the problems of banking and credit were discussed.[46] As a solution to the problems of farm credit, and credit for the man of limited means, Page cited the example of the European co-operative credit banks as a method of spreading opportunity and thus, democracy. The expansion of credit to small enterprise might make more men independent of organized labor, and lessen the inevitability of a class struggle. Page continued to decry "class thought" but had to admit that a distinct pattern of working class thought had emerged.[47]

In addition to the usual financial, educational business and health topics, The World's Work during 1912 explored the rise of Socialism, at home and abroad.[48] There was heightened concern with ways and means of purifying American society, which was manifested by articles on the high cost of living, the economic value of good roads, the return of ethics to business through public action against the trusts, the world-wide control of disease, the failure of the Pure Food and Drug Act, the efforts of women's organizations and the potential place of cooperatives, agricultural and commercial, in the American economic system.

The "Progressive" impulse manifested by The World's Work was, however, a cautious one. "The public mind," wrote Page, "is concerning itself, as perhaps never before, with fundamental and constructive things. It is wary of the sensational. It is tired of mere criticism. It is disgusted with abuse, whether in politics or in other personal scrambles. It is done with 'muckraking'." Page thus undertook editorially an explanation of "What a Constructive Progressive Plan in Politics Means," specifically, the movement of public opinion toward more direct and more responsible government.[49]

Following the Presidential election of 1912, portions of Woodrow Wilson's The New Freedom, printed in special type, were featured serially in The World's Work. These excerpts ran from January, 1913 to April, 1913. As if to point up the values stressed by Wilson, Page ran a fictional series about a businessman which pointed up thrift, honesty, hardwork, judgement and experience as being the proper qualities for business

success. This series was a paean to competition, in
which true ability, merit and a public service
orientation led to personal success. It ran con-
currently with Woodrow Wilson's The New Freedom and
another series entitled "The Battle Line of Labor",
presenting a rounded picture of the limits of Page's
progressivism.[50]

The move toward longer range planning of The
World's Work, noticeable after 1908 and completed in
1911, left Page with more time to pursue his outside
interests or simply to relax. Arthur Wilson Page,
Walter Page's second son had become managing editor in
1911, and Page had acquired a dependable staff which
included such men as C.M. Keys and William Bayard
Hale. More and more, speaking tours or meetings on
behalf of Southern education had taken Page away from
Garden City. He also traveled on behalf of the
magazine throughout his tenure as editor, especially
to fairs and expositions. Such travels were in line
with his stated philosophy that: "The real work of
making a 'live' magazine cannot be done in the
office."[51]

As time went on, Page spent more time resting, or
attending to affairs in North Carolina. Page and his
wife spent March and part of April in the South in
both 1912 and 1913. The remainder of 1912, Page was
active in the press promotion of Woodrow Wilson's
nomination and election.[52]

In retrospect, The World's Work's enthusiasm for
Wilson is clear, but nothing like it might have been,
had Page given in to his inner desires. In part, Page
attributed this restraint to differences of opinion
among the staff and owners of The World's Work. "The
policy of the magazine," he wrote, "was determined by
the editor, who is the court of last appeal. There
were in the group some men who differed with the
political policy of the magazine. What better correc-
tive influence against sheer partisanship could be
devised?"[53] Page realized that too great an identifi-
cation with Wilson's campaign might affect the revenue
of The World's Work. He also distrusted what he had
called editorially "men's burning enthusiasm" and had
thus always eschewed immoderate statements. In those
areas of his greatest interest, philanthropy in the
South, universal education, agriculture and Woodrow
Wilson, Page's prose was consistently dispassionate to
a fault.

During and after the election, Page involved himself in writing memoranda for Wilson, outlining agriculture policy and avoiding the appearance of seeking office. On election day, November 5, 1912, Page wrote to Wilson outlining some of his hopes for action by the new administration in the areas of agriculture and credit.[54] During an interview with President-elect Wilson on November 15, 1912, Page was asked to offer some comments and opinions as to who should be the new Secretary of Agriculture. In addition, Page was asked to write briefs on the Bureau of Education, the Rural Credit Societies, conservation and the Department of Agriculture. These were submitted to Wilson before the end of the month.[55]

Page's interest in agriculture was so great that naturally, he hoped to influence the choice of Secretary of Agriculture. Whether he sought the position himself is a matter of some doubt. At least, the experience of others in seeking office directly from Wilson had been disastrous. One advisor of long standing, William F. McCombs, had lost all association with Wilson by suggesting that Wilson owed him a place in the cabinet.[56]

Page's letter to Wilson, stating that he was not interested in being Secretary of Agriculture, contains some interesting contradictions. First of all, for a man who wrote "one draft" editorials, suitable, according to his partner F.N. Doubleday for direct submission to the printer,[57] the draft of the letter to Wilson is almost incomprehensible because of deletions and corrections. Secondly, after stating that "I have never had this nor any such thing in mind," Page offers far too many reasons why he is unsuited to the job, thereby indicating that he had indeed thought about the possibility. Finally, the letter is especially delicate, considering the personal relationship already established between Page and Wilson and the early and effective efforts of Page toward Wilson's election.[58]

Arthur Link has suggested that "the only hope for preferment lay in assiduously avowing that they did not want the office they had set their hearts upon."[59] To Henry Wallace, the Iowa farm editor who had indicated his belief that Page was the best man for the Agriculture Department, Page wrote that he would not presume to advise the President unless requested to do so. "As for me," Page continued, "I doubt if he ever thought of that; and of course, I should never put it in his head. Nothing, I think, will ever come of your flattering thought of me and of the same suggestion that keeps coming from all sorts of sources. In fact, I should be willing to take the job (if it should be offered, as I have no idea it ever will be) only to keep it from going to some politician or to some professor. Neither of those types of men can do it."[60]

Page's interest in politics and public service, exhibited both through his journalistic efforts and his work on the various education boards, was built upon his belief, that men of public spirit, intelligence and refinement had a positive duty to enter politics. And of course, "We are all politicians at bottom."[61] Despite his journalistic humility, Page enjoyed the limelight. His availability as a speaker is one indication of this. His long fight for editorial control of his own magazine is another.

It is ironic that Page, who by interest and knowledge was well suited to be Secretary of Agriculture, got his reward in an area where his blunt honesty was a drawback. Indeed, Page had always exhibited a broad interest in foreign affairs, even though The World's Work had sharply curtailed that aspect of its coverage after 1908. On April 1, 1913, Colonel Edward M. House called to advise Page that President Wilson wanted him to accept the post of Ambassador to England. Page admitted his lack of knowledge of the duties, but he desired a rest from editorial work and saw positive social advantages to members of his family. In addition, Page liked to be out among the men who were doing things, and as Ambassador, he "could test himself against men of consequence."[62]

As had become his custom, Page took his wife to Pinehurst, North Carolina for the entire month of February, 1913. He returned to his editorial duties during March, and after the April 1, 1913 call from Colonel House, he virtually relinquished his editorial duties altogether to his son, Arthur. In April, Page journeyed to Washington, D.C. for diplomatic orientation, thence to Richmond, Virginia, where he presided over the Southern Educational Conference, and finally home to Garden City, New York, where numerous groups gave farewell dinners and receptions for him and Mrs. Page.[63]

It has been suggested by Ross Gregory, one of the most recent commentators on Page's ambassadorial years, that Walter Page's writings and especially his later writings were done with the historian in mind.[64] To a large extent, this seems to be true. A diary note, made on January 9, 1911, discussed the possibility of a family history. "All my manuscripts - publish or destroy!" scribbled Page. "Publish the best, each in a small volume."[65] Without doubt, this notation was never intended for the historian's view.

For the most part, Page's public and private statements were remarkably consistent. The World's Work reflected quite accurately his opinions on the subjects with which it dealt. Certain selectivity, notably in what The World's Work did not contain, only illustrates Page's desire to concentrate upon those subjects which interested him most. Fortunately, he was interested in practically everything. Even his behind the scenes political activity during 1912, when he never let it be publicly known that he was part of Wilson's publicity committee, showed editorial integrity. His preference for Woodrow Wilson was obvious. No previous Presidential candidate was ever so fully endorsed in the pages of The World's Work. Only the extent of Page's dedication to Wilson's election was not stated.

From the first issue, in November of 1900, the purpose and tone of The World's Work was set. Through whatever changes in content and emphasis that occurred during Page's thirteen years as editor, that purpose remained consistent. The economic success of The World's Work testifies to the fact that Page's editorial formula had found a reading public amenable to the "interpretation of the important achievements of contemporaneous life" and to "the literature of action."[66]

Walter Page repeated his purpose, usually in brief anniversary editorials. Near the end of his tenure, in January, 1913, he repeated once more his views of what a good magazine ought to be.

> The first principle is that every
> piece published shall be interest-
> ing....The aim is...to report and
> interpret representative activities
> of our time...to give the reader a
> well-proportioned knowledge of what
> sort of things are happening in the
> world--in the American world in

particular....it is a cheerful and
exhilarating occupation....The real
reward of the editorial life is in
the friends and acquaintances that
one has occasion...to make....We
must go about the United States and
see what men are doing.... it is
interesting work...the main thing
to be said about it is that it is
work, unceasing, hard work.[67]

Page was pleased that the audience of The World's
Work came from all walks of life. He was doubly
pleased that some articles describing work in education
or sanitation had inspired groups to copy the methods
and goals described therein. "The results," he wrote,
"that justify the magazine's existence are what educational folk...call 'inspirational'."

Making a successful magazine, he continued,
"required...balanced judgement, an intellectual inability to be drawn...to allow one's personal tastes and
particular enthusiasms to dominate the whole periodical....Common sense is the most useful quality that
you can get into an editorial office." Furthermore,
the finding of men who can write with directness and
warmth was essential. Page claimed to have spent ten
years assembling the four key staff writers who made
the bulk of the magazine. In the end, he wrote, "the
successful editing of such a magazine is in reality
the interpretation of the people, their revelation to
themselves... This is what with all humility and
earnestness we are trying to do."[68]

Thus, at the end of Page's tenure as editor, as
in the beginning, the purpose was the same. The
editorial outlook changed, but mostly in emphasis, not
in content. This purpose was to instruct the public,
in the opportunities of industry and agriculture; in
the values of democracy as Page interpreted them; and,
in the practical necessities of education and personal
health. In this purpose, Page was consistent from
beginning to end. It is in the internal analysis of
the various topics which dominated the magazine that
conflicting ideas and values are found. These ideas
and values while purporting to be in the best interest
of America were often contradictory, negative and even
destructive of ideal human values.

[1]Walter Hines Page, "Emphasizing the Higher Life," The World's Work, X (July, 1905), 6346.

[2]The World's Work, VII (November, 1903).

[3]Walter Hines Page, "On A Tenth Birthday," The World's Work, XXI (January, 1911), 13903-17.

[4]See articles on the insurance industry by "O.P." in The World's Work from November, 1905 to April, 1906.

[5]The World's Work, VII (April, 1904). The magazine carried discussions of the important battles and developments through the settlement of the war in the spring of 1905. Page's admiration of Japanese efficiency was very evident.

[6]Isaac F. Marcosson, Adventures in Interviewing (New York, 1919), p. 42. See also the introduction to the 1923 edition of A Publisher's Confession, Frank Nelson Doubleday's introductory statements on Walter Hines Page.

[7]Edwin Mims, "Walter Hines Page: Friend of the South," The South Atlantic Quarterly, XVIII (April, 1919), 110-111.

[8]Dr. Woods Hutchinson, "The Mongolian As A Working-man," The World's Work, XIV (September, 1907), 9372-76. Page accepted the then prevailing view that some racial-national groups were superior to others. In addition to the obvious superiority of the white race over the yellow, brown and black peoples, there were definite rankings among the all white racial-national groups. Page, however, was not especially virulent about racial distinctions, accepting them as givens, not actively promoting them. His passive approach to white superiority was one element of his estrangement from Southern spokesmen such as Josephus Daniels.

[9]Walter Hines Page, "The Presidential Year and its Outlook," The World's Work, XV (January, 1908), 9725.

[10]Robert Bridges, "Woodrow Wilson, President of Princeton," The World's Work, XV (January, 1908),

9792-97.

[11]Walter Hines Page, "Mr. Rockefeller's Reminiscences," The World's Work, XVI (July, 1908), 10417-18.

[12]Peter Lyon, Success Story: The Life and Times of S.S. McClure (New York, 1963), p. 214. Ida Tarbell's series on the Standard Oil Company began in November, 1902 and ran sporadically until October, 1904.

[13]Walter Hines Page, "The Archbold-Foraker Letters," The World's Work, XVII (November, 1908), 10851-53; Frank Luther Mott, A History of American Magazines, IV (Cambridge, Mass., 1957), 777.

[14]Walter Hines Page, "A Word to the Standard Oil Company," The World's Work, XVII (November, 1908), 10854-54.

[15]See articles in The World's Work, XXI (November, 1910) by James J. Hill and C.M. Keys for a clear exposition of the nature, purpose and destiny of railroads from opposite points of view.

[16]Frank Luther Mott, A History of American Magazines, IV (Cambridge, Mass., 1957), 777. Mott is correct in his assertion that Page was consistent in his views, i.e., not a liberal before 1906 and a conservative afterward. However, Mott's use of the Foraker-Archbold letters, as against the Rockefeller reminiscences, is inappropriate proof of Page's so-called "balanced viewpoint" editorial policy. Mott is right, but for the wrong reasons. Furthermore, Page never really attacked the "system". Rather, he pointed out the immorality of the men who ran the system, often appearing more disappointed than horrified.

[17]Theodore Roosevelt to Walter Hines Page, August 10, 1908, Page MSS, Harvard.

[18]Undated memo, presumably prepared for President-elect Woodrow Wilson, Page MSS, Harvard.

[19]Walter Hines Page, "The Entrenchments of Privilege," The World's Work, XVIII (June, 1909), 11623.

[20]Walter Hines Page, "Important Plans for The World's Work," The World's Work, XVIII (October, 1909), 12093-25.

[21]Ibid.

[22]There were only 109 pages of text in November, 1909 as opposed to the original 116 pages of text.

[23]"Roosevelt Again," The World's Work, XX (July, 1910), 13124-38, unsigned.

[24]The World's Work, XX (August, 1910), 13259-85.

[25]Walter Hines Page, "Planting a Publishing House in the Country," The World's Work, XX (October, 1910), 13480.

[26]Walter Hines Page, "Ten Years of The World's Work," The World's Work, XXI (January, 1911), 13905.

[27]Ibid., p. 13910.

[28]Ibid., p. 13915.

[29]Arthur Wilson Page, "A Cotton-Harvester at Last," The World's Work, XXI (December, 1910), 13748-60; Page Diary, September, 1911 and 1912, Page MSS, Harvard.

[30]Walter Hines Page, "Ten Years of The World's Work," The World's Work, XXI (January, 1911), 13906-07.

[31]The School of Tomorrow; a collection of prize essays from The World's Work (Garden City, New York, 1911).

[32]Henry Oyen, "Down to the Slums," The World's Work, XXI (March, 1911), 14101-12; "In the Slum," XXI (April, 1911), 14275-82; "Up From the Slum," XXII (May, 1911), 14374-83.

[33]Walter Hines Page, "A Word About Revolutions," The World's Work, XXII (August, 1911), 14668. The articles by George Perkins appeared in The World's Work, XXII (June, 1911), 11465-71; XXII (July, 1911), 14619-25.

[34]Walter Hines Page, "Really Great Days in Congress," The World's Work, XXII (August, 1911, 14675-76.

[35]Walter Hines Page, "The Talk of The Office," The World's Work, XXII (October, 1911), Advertising Section.

[36]Walter Hines Page, "A New Dress and Other New Things," _The World's Work_, XXII (October, 1911), 14921.

[37]The Editors [Walter Hines Page], "The March of the Cities," _The World's Work_, XXIII (November, 1911), 118. This feature continued as long as Page remained editor, and several months into the tenure of his son, Arthur Wilson Page.

[38]_The Southerner: Being the Autobiography of Nicholas Worth_ (New York, 1909). This novel, written anonymously by Walter Hines Page, first appeared serially in _The Atlantic Monthly_ and was published by Doubleday, Page & Company in 1909. This was Page's only attempt at a novel. It was allegorical, and highly didactic.

[39]Walter Hines Page to Wallace Buttrick, August 18, 1911, Page MSS, Harvard.

[40]Walter Hines Page, "Does Anybody Really Want a Farm?" _The World's Work_, XXIII (November, 1911), 119.

[41]_The School of Tomorrow_: a collection of prize essays from _The World's Work_ (Garden City, New York, 1911).

[42]Walter Hines Page, "Does Anybody Want a Farm? The Answer," _The World's Work_, XXIII (January, 1912), 352-355.

[43]Walter Hines Page, "The Choosing of a Farm," _The World's Work_, XXIII (March, 1912), 598.

[44]Walter Hines Page, "The Great Country Life Movement," _The World's Work_, XXIII (April, 1912), 616-619.

[45]Walter Hines Page to Ray Stannard Baker, February 23, 1912, Page MSS, Harvard. The platforms of the candidates appeared in _The World's Work_ [unsigned], XXIV (May, 1912), 20. Page had supported William Howard Taft prior to 1909 when Taft ran into trouble with Congress over the tariff revision. Thereafter, Page found him too indecisive. As for the re-emergence of Theodore Roosevelt, another President whom Page had supported in his day, Page stated in a March, 1912 editorial entitled "Mr. Roosevelt?" that the "natural nominees of the two parties...would be President Taft and Governor Wilson. One represents the bewildered inefficiency of one party, and the other the best

aspirations of the other party in its hope of rejuvenation.

The call for Mr. Roosevelt must be classed not a normal and calm but excited and mistaken act of desperation, national tradition and to a patriotic resolution of his own, and a humiliating and ominous confession of impending defeat." [XXIII (March, 1912), 489-491]

A six part series on Woodrow Wilson appeared in The World's Work in October, 1911 and ran through March of 1912. In September, 1912, there appeared a comparison of Wilson, Taft and Roosevelt by "A Common Acquaintance." The article was quite kind to Taft, derogatory to Roosevelt and laudatory of Wilson. ["Wilson-Taft-Roosevelt", XXIV (September, 1912), 569-575.]

[46]Charles Francis Adams, "Pensions: Worse and More of Them," The World's Work, XXIII (December, 1911), 189-196; Ibid. (January, 1912), 327-334; Ibid. (February, 1912), 385-398.

[47]Walter Hines Page, "A Class War," The World's Work, XXIII (April, 1912), 611.

[48]This was done in a five part series by Samual P. Orth, running from May, 1912 through September, 1912.

[49]Walter Hines Page, "A Few Announcements," The World's Work, XXIV (September, 1912), 501-502.

[50]Edward Mott Woolley, "Addison Broadhurst, Master Merchant," The World's Work, XXV (January, 1913), 351-356; Ibid. (February, 1913), 469-476; Ibid. (March, 1913), 591-597; Ibid. (April, 1913), 708-715; Samuel P. Orth, "The Battle Line of Labor," XXV (November, 1912), 49-61; Ibid. (December, 1912), 197-205; Ibid. (January, 1913), 275-285; Ibid. (February, 1913), 431-437.

[51]Walter Hines Page, "What The World's Work is Trying To Do," The World's Work, XXV (January, 1913), 265.

[52]Page Diary, 1912, Page MSS, Harvard.

[53]Walter Hines Page, "What The World's Work is Trying To Do," The World's Work, XXV (January, 1913), 266. See also note #45 above.

[54]Walter Hines Page to Woodrow Wilson, November 12, 1912, Page MSS, Harvard.

[55]Memorandum, Page MSS, Harvard; Burton J. Hendrick, The Life and Letters of Walter Hines Page, (New York, 1923), Vol. I, 112; Frederick B. Weaver, "Walter Hines Page and the Progressive Mood," unpublished doctoral dissertation, (University of North Carolina, Chapel Hill), pp. 246-247.

[56]Arthur Link, Wilson, II: The New Freedom (Princeton, New Jersey, 1956), 5.

[57]Frank Nelson Doubleday's Introduction to the 1923 edition of Walter Hines Page, A Publisher's Confession.

[58]Walter Hines Page to Woodrow Wilson, undated, but presumed to have been written in late November, 1912, Page MSS, Harvard. See also Weaver, "Walter Hines Page and the Progressive Mood," pp. 235-244 for the extent of Page's and Wilson's personal relationship. Wilson chose Doubleday, Page & Company to publish The New Freedom. See Weaver, pp. 245-251 for details of Page's efforts to influence Wilson's choice of the Secretary of Agriculture.

[59]Link, Wilson, p. 7.

[60]Walter Hines Page to Henry Wallace, November 16, 1912, Page MSS, Harvard. President-elect Wilson had requested on November 15, 1912, the day before this letter, that Page offer some thoughts on who should fill the position of Secretary of Agriculture. Interestingly, despite his comment to Wallace that the post should not go to "some professor," Page included Professor Charles Van Hise, President of the University of Wisconsin, in his list of recommendations to President Wilson.

[61]Walter Hines Page, "We are all Politicians at Bottom," The World's Work, XXIII (January, 1912), 243.

[62]Page Diary, section entitled "The Ambassadorship," Page MSS, Harvard. This account appears to have been written for the historian. While April 1, 1913 may have been the official notification date, Page was approached much earlier according to the account of Colonel Edward M. House, the man who supposedly made the official offer of the Ambassadorship on behalf of President Wilson.

[63]Page Diary, "The Ambassadorship," and Page datebook for 1913, Page MSS, Harvard.

[64]Ross Gregory, <u>Walter Hines Page: Ambassador to the Court of St. James</u> (Lexington, Kentucky, 1970).

[65]Page Diary, January 9, 1911, Page MSS, Harvard. The dating of such notations is liable to be deceptive. The year cited can be, for the most part, counted upon. The month cited also. However, many of Page's diary notations encompass two or more pages, so that the accuracy of individual days is highly problematical. It appears that Page often used pocket diaries more as notation pads than as date books, although he did refer specifically to exact dates in many notations.

[66]Walter Hines Page, untitled editorial, <u>The World's Work</u>, I (April, 1901), 584.

[67]Walter Hines Page, "What <u>The World's Work</u> is Trying To Do," <u>The World's Work</u>, XXV (January, 1913), 265-268.

[68]<u>Ibid</u>.

CHAPTER IV

WALTER HINES PAGE AND THE PROBLEM OF THE
"NEW IMMIGRATION": THE PROGRESSIVE AS RACIST

The "problem" of immigration, as viewed by Americans in the period between 1895 and 1920, reflected long-standing racial distinctions based not only on color but also upon national-racial characteristics and pseudoscientific nostrums. In almost no other area of national life was there so much intellectual confusion. In short, imperfect knowledge of the real nature of genetic characteristics made it possible for individuals to internalize completely antithetical beliefs. Being deeply intertwined with current racial shibboleths, immigration during the Progressive period appeared to threaten the basic values of capitalism and democracy.

Like most other educated Americans, Walter Hines Page could not escape the belief systems of his day. Even a man whose racism was as moderated as was Page's could not find a position upon the immigration question which, because of racial attitudes, was not inherently self-contradictory.

Immigration was, and had always been, a fact of American life. Until the late 1840's, immigration had no negative connotations. Thereafter, it was viewed by some as a potential problem; by others as the basis of our national strength. However, after 1877, immigration was viewed increasingly as a problem, not only because of the changing origin of the immigrants, but also for economic and political reasons.

One of the more important ramifications of the "new immigration" was the growing concern that the inferior racial stock, the Jews, Italians and Slavs then coming to America, would seriously weaken the "American race." There was, of course, no real agreement upon what constituted the "American race" other than that it had sprung from Anglo-Saxon, Teutonic or Nordic immigrants and was now tempered with some Irish blood. In the economic realm, there was the effect of immigration upon wage rates, the loss of American capital through immigrants sending or taking back to Europe several hundred million dollars per year, the weakening of labor unions because of the immigrant labor surplus and basic immigrant disinterest in unions. In the area of social development, the immigrant was believed to be both the

cause of slums, and increasingly unassimilable into
American society. This latter aspect was in turn due to
a high level of illiteracy, sickness and ignorance.
Politically, the immigrant was the tool of the "bosses,"
and thus doubly the enemy of clean government and urban
purity. Immigrants were also viewed as tending toward
collectivist activities, ranging from basic unionism
to the more subversive Socialist ideals.

The basic problem for most anti-immigrationists in
this period was not simply that the tide of immigration
was too great, but that the quality of the immigrant
had become severely degraded. The belief that assimilation of these seemingly inferior national-racial groups
was possible faltered in the face of sheer numbers.
There was a new awareness of important social problems
which immigration supposedly caused. First, there was
the problem of city government, especially in the North-
east, where manipulation of the immigrant vote was seen
as being the basis of continuing rule by corrupt bosses.
To be sure, the naturalization procedures were so loose
as to invite abuses in the granting of citizenship,
and certainly new immigrants contributed strongly to the
support of existing power structures such as Tammany
Hall in New York City.

Secondly, slums were believed to be the creation
of immigrants, instead of being attributed to the greed
of landlords. The immigrants were blamed because they
did not all display cleanliness and thrift. "They were
poor because they were depraved" was the judgment, and
their ignorance and willingness to work for lower wages
was inimical to the preservation of native American
economic ideals. In short, the European immigrant was
judged, after he ceased to be from the North of Europe,
to be a major cause of the very municipal problems
which the Progressive movement found most repulsive.

Objections to immigration, while heightened in the
early years of the new century, were nothing new. The
Irish invasion of the 1840's brought forth "Know-Noth-
ingism." The great railroad strike of 1877 elicited
hidden fears of European radicalism, and led to pressure
to restrict the free flow of immigrants. In the 1890's
and into the 20th Century, the primary objections were
based on "scientific" theories of race.

Statistical articles bore out the fact that the
increasing tide of immigration was coming from Southern
and Eastern Europe. The World's Work stated in 1902:

Roughly speaking, the North-of-Europe
people make better citizens than those
from the South of Europe. The better
class go to the country and the worst
to the cities. The Greeks are considered about the least desirable of all;
the Italians from the Southern portion
of the peninsula also make poor citizens;
but those from the northern part of Italy
rank with the Swiss and other desirable
nationalities. From 1821 to 1900,
according to a recent Census Bulletin,
over 19,000,000 immigrants landed in
the United States. Germany sent
5,000,000; Ireland, 3,870,000; Great
Britain, 3,026,000; Scandinavia,
1,246,000; Austria-Hungary (including
Bohemia), 1,000,000; and Italy,
1,000,000. Once the stream came from
the North of Europe; now it comes
chiefly from the South--from the undesirable countries.[1]

This viewpoint was not much removed from the racial
theories of Count Arthur de Gobineau, who postulated
in his Essay in 1856 that there were distinct and
important differences between the "Nordic" and the
"Latin" races. The "Nordic" peoples, in his view, were
vastly superior, and destined to rule all the others.
His racial theories were seminal for much of the racial
theory which developed during the second half of the
19th Century. Despite the supposed undesirability of
immigrants from the South of Europe, the idea was not
to "forbid all people from coming," but to invoke some
form of rational restriction in conjunction with foreign
governments.[2]

"Rational restriction," a rational approach to the
problem, and, if possible, rational solutions. This
would be the editorial approach of Walter Hines Page.
He solicited articles on immigration, allowing a wide
range of opinions, contradictions and equivocations.
Some immigration articles in The World's Work were more
exclusionist than others. Some favored the melting pot
theory, while others stressed the unassimilable aspect
of the new European immigration. Some tried to do both
at the same time. Page's own editorials toyed with
stronger restrictions than were then currently in force
but he could never bring himself to endorse a complete
shutoff of immigration. He always sought ways of

accepting the best and eliminating the worst of the immigrants.

Perhaps the whole editorial policy is neatly summed up in the first immigration article to appear in The World's Work. Aptly titled, "The Changing Nature of Immigration," the article statistically cited the changes in the source of immigration, pointing out that the trend was even more fearful than had previously been thought. "The statistics of immigration for successive years," the author stated, "would be even more significant....if the present system of classifying arrivals according to race as well as to country of residence had been adopted sooner." The "national" system of counting had masked the "noticeable feature in recent immigration....the predominance of three racial stocks, usually considered of doubtful social and industrial value, the Slavs, the Italians and the Hebrews. Our problem is now the problem of the Italian, the Jew and the Slav--no longer of the Irishman and the German."

Despite its harsh judgment, the article credited immigrants with cleanliness and honesty, and noted with some satisfaction that at least the new immigration came mostly from the countryside, and hadn't brought the vices of European urban life. The rural virtues, however, were soon lost in the American urban setting, as the new immigrant became the victim of the dregs of previous immigration which still inhabited the slums.

The author, Kate Holladay Claghorn, exhibited great faith in the melting pot ideal. Despite the "doubtful social and industrial value" of the Slav, the Jew and the Italian....somehow, in haphazard ways, we assimilate them....the children of almost any kind of parents become American." The author sidesteps the importance of "race," the very basis of her article, by suggesting that it is the attitudes and values which are brought from the old world, rather than the national origins which appear to make the differences. Also, because of their rural origins, the new immigrants are more moral; and, hence, more acceptable than immigrants from European cities. The Jews, of course, were city dwellers, but their "circumstances were peculiar."[3] Either the changing origins of immigration made a difference or it didn't. Neither Page nor the authors from whom he solicited articles on immigration could ever really make up their minds.

The majority of Page's own editorial comments

dealt with Jewish immigration, with Anglo-Saxon supremacy worldwide and methods of keeping out the worst
elements of immigration while utilizing the best elements for national growth. Page firmly believed that
there was room for many more immigrants in the American
countryside, and he pursued ways of getting immigrants
from rural backgrounds directly into the American
countryside without the apparently inevitable stop in
urban slums. He also dealt with the problems of oriental immigration. Here, because racial inferiority
was presumed, Page let his economic nationalism over-
ride his sense of racial nationalism. He advocated
limited Chinese immigration for economic purposes,
never intending that any attempt at assimilation take
place. For economic reasons also, Page was more concerned with not insulting the Japanese than with advocating their total exclusion. Page's attitude toward
immigration restriction changed from relative unconcern
in 1900 to support for more stringent restrictions by
1912.

Throughout his tenure as editor of The World's
Work, Page continued to believe in the superiority of
the Anglo-Saxon peoples. These were, and were destined
to remain, the leaders of the world. Of the three
major English-speaking nations--England, America, and
Australia--the Americans were destined to become supreme
because of their democratic institutions. "That the
English race in a democracy," Page wrote, "should out-
strip the English race in an aristocratic society was to
us a foregone conclusion a hundred years ago. Freedom
of opportunity and democracy will make the men who live
under it more efficient than the men who live under an
aristocracy....these are the simple and fundamental
facts that determine the future domination of the
world." [4]

At least during the first year of The World's
Work's existence, Page did not share the fears of
those who believed that the Anglo-Saxon stock in America
was being weakened. He commented upon the large number
of English immigrants that had come to America since
the 1850's. Discounting the Scottish and Irish, 53% of
the total emigration from the British Isles since 1853
had been English. "The interesting fact," he wrote,
"....is that we continue to be English in blood by new
immigration, and we are not such a motley crew as we
are sometimes told that we are." [5] This optimism, however, was a matter of degree only, as the changing
nature of immigration had already been noted by The

For Page, one of the most controversial aspects of the new immigration was the Russian Jew. Over the years, Page solicited a variety of opinions on the nature of the Jew in America and the possibility of his assimilation.[7] Page himself was not optimistic about the Jewish capacity for assimilation into American life. His first actual statement on American Jewry appeared in October, 1902. He posed the question of the potentiality of Jewish assimilation, stating:

> It is a pertinent and interesting
> inquiry whether they will persist as
> a distinct race under Republican in-
> stitutions as they have for so many
> centuries under persecution in the
> Old World.

Religion, "apparently their strongest bond," had become liberalized by life in America. "Still, the race feeling remains strong even after religious differences have practically disappeared." The social distinctions, based upon mutual prejudice, remained persistent and might even be growing.

> Taken all in all, the Jew is at home
> in the United States. He is not
> persecuted here. But he both suffers
> and practices social exclusion. He
> acquires some of the American vices,
> but even these have not eradicated
> his race feeling. He becomes an
> ardent American, but he remains a Jew.

It was, Page suggested, too early to tell if total assimilation could occur, but he hoped that the Jews would "contribute,...genius and....physical tenacity to the common mass."[8]

Page's editorial statement is basically quite mild when compared with public attitudes toward the Jews in 1902. Page's private feelings about Jews were somewhat stronger, perhaps due in part to his experience as editor of the Forum. In an attempt to gain control over the Forum, Page became involved in protracted litigation with the other owners, some of whom were Jewish. "Once the contest was engaged it took the form in Page's mind of a conspiracy by 'Jews' of the ordinary commercial type" to cheat him out of his property.[9]

To a friend in 1895, Page wrote that:

> There is no use blinking the central
> truth of the whole situation, which
> is this--that the whole controversy
> turns on the race feeling. Our
> Hebrew friends, who are very emo-
> tional and clannish, when they saw
> the Forum a thing of power and with-
> in sight of prosperity, wished the
> glory of it or the money to be got
> from it if they should sell it. In
> spite of the fact that its power and
> profit and the assurance of its
> future were brought about by my work
> and money of the preferred stockholders,
> they have themselves drawn the race
> line.... This group of Hebrew gentle-
> men cannot conduct the Forum. They
> have no broad or proper knowledge of
> American character, or nationality,
> or aspiration--not even of our
> institutions. [10]

In correspondence with Horace Scudder, editor of
the Atlantic Monthly, Page wrote that the laydown of
the Forum had been sudden and he had no plans for the
future when he resigned. "There was," he wrote to
Scudder, "a considerable financial interest in the Forum
held by 'Hebrews' and certain conditions that arose
from that fact gave him the choice to resign or lose
his self-respect. He was not overcome by weariness," he
said, but rather by "the unaromatic odors from the back
alleys of Jerusalem." [11]

These deeper feelings regarding Jews appeared
occasionally in editorials specifically on Jewish
immigration, but were usually tempered in editorials
where the topic was the total question of immigration.
In the latter case, it was difficult for Page to turn
his back on people who immigrated because of simple
hope for a better life. He was, however, angered by
forced immigration, caused by the driving out of un-
wanted peoples by European nations, because this brought
to America a type of immigrant of low ambition and
ability. In the latter years of the Nineteenth Century,
and into the Twentieth Century, Russia was a prime
offender in this regard.

In November, 1902, Page commented upon a problem

caused by an American note to Rumania requesting that they cease granting passports to Jews. Rumania, harsh in its persecution of Jews, maintained that theirs was an economic conflict, that the Jews "if left unrestricted, so get the better of the peasants in all economic ways as to reduce them to poverty." Secretary Hay's note of protest, while having the salutary effect of stopping Rumanian Jewish emmigration to the United States, made the lot of the Jews in Rumania much harsher. Of course, the note called to the world's attention the inhumane treatment of the Jews, also embarrassing Russia and Austria-Hungary, the powers who guaranteed Rumania's good conduct. Most important for Page, "All Europe has been informed of our unwillingness to receive undesirable immigrants--to be a dumping ground for a population that nobody wants."[12]

Page believed that more restriction of immigration was necessary. To cut corruption out of American life required that the most degenerate and ignorant of the European immigrants be denied entry. Otherwise, American values and native American stock would be mongrelized and corrupted, and the American race weakened beyond redemption.

For these reasons, Page personally rejected the "settlement house" approach, although he printed articles which supported that view.[13] Its advocates were characterized by their desire to preserve the cultural values of immigrant groups while attempting to assimilate them politically and socially. Settlement house advocates often found the anti-immigration forces too extreme, and held stubbornly to their belief in America as the melting pot. For Page, as for the more militant anti-immigrationists, the melting pot theory was doubly dangerous because the elements to be assimilated were of increasingly inferior material.

Page also struggled with the literacy test devices which had the support of the Anti-Immigration League during the early years of the Twentieth Century. These he found to be ineffective against the Jews, because they managed to educate a much higher percentage of their people than either the Italian peasant or the Slavic peoples. Literacy tests favored the Northern European immigrant, but few of these were ever turned away anyhow, and after 1900 they made up only a small percentage of the total immigration.[14] Still, literacy requirements were better than nothing at all.

Thus, Page was not terribly pleased with the revisions in the immigration laws which occurred in 1903 because they contained no literacy or educational qualifications. Generally, he stated, the new law "freely admits every proper person from any land--we shall still have refuge to the oppressed and opportunity to the ambitious. But whether it will exclude all the unfit whom the Old World governments assist to come, or whom energetic steamship agents procure, is doubtful."[15] Page pointed to Immigration Restriction League estimates that of the 650,000 arrivals in 1902, 28% were illiterate, and 44% of those from Southern Europe were illiterates. In his opinion, the new law would not bar many more immigrants because "illiteracy was not made a bar to entry....The effort will be continued so to amend the law as to require an educational qualification for admission."[16]

World events tended to dictate the content of the editorial pages of The World's Work. However, the lesson to be learned from events, as revealed by Page, could be quite revealing of his personal concerns. For example, Page discussed, in mid-1903, a recent Jewish massacre in Russia. The cause was laid in part to Jewish "hard dealing and in part to the oppressive legal restrictions which forced the Jew to become 'troublesome' and to develop a 'hard character'." His condemnation of such massacres was based on the view that such actions only stimulated emigration to America. He pointed out also that given the Jewish preference for marriage "only within their own race," their racial "identity" and their "compactness, will our democracy be able to last to assimilate them? Will they ever be merged in our composite races?"[17] Page concluded that the sending of money to relieve the distress of the Jews in Russia could only encourage them to emigrate to America. It should be done anyway, but at the same time we should make sure that our immigration laws were rigidly enforced.

Also during 1903, for the first time in The World's Work, Page made the connection between immigration and urban problems. He admitted that while the Jews "do not become public charges....when they come in great swarms they do become a grave social burden to our great cities." In the same editorial, he stumped for greater immigration restrictions, pointing out that an American policy of easy financial relief and open immigration tended to encourage other European nations to employ harsh measures against the Jews to drive them to

America. "The humane impulses of American citizens," he wrote, "may easily be turned to assisting undesirable immigration."[18]

Despite his opposition to Jewish immigration on a large scale, Page wrote in early 1906 that "we have no Jewish question. Certainly not like Europe's." In America, the Jew had prospered, had developed into "the best practical man of his race and proved his value to the country." The Jews had suffered from "a few annoyances that spring from race feeling. It would be idle to deny that they both give and receive annoyances; and doubtless they always will so long as they remain a separate race....so long as the marriage of Jews and Christians does not become common.... They have been willing to take advantage of the toleration and of the opportunities given by a democracy, but.... they are not willing to lose their identity in the people....Race is stronger than nationality--by far."

Page further suggested that an influx of Russian Jewish immigrants might increase the opportunities for mutual annoyance. He again admitted that the Jew in America was an economic asset, seldom a cause of public expense. However, Page reflected the then current social view that it was solely the Jew's stubbornness in clinging to his own people and faith that frustrated assimilation.[19]

Not only the Jew, but the Italians, with their proclivity for remaining in the cities, vastly complicated the problems of the already overburdened city governments. Page was not specific on this point, but suggested that these immigrants brought their background as "an oppressed and unfortunate class" from the Old World cities, and essentially, Page blamed the immigrants for the creation of slums, imputing that slums were first found in European cities. Our cities, given our "new country and abundance of land," should have been able to avoid problems which plagued the Old World for centuries past. "But instead of this happy result," said Page, "we are going through the experience of Europe partly because Europe empties its slums and ghettos into our cities; and the new high-tide of immigration of people who huddle in our already most densely populated areas constantly makes our city problems more difficult."[20]

Page's solution to this problem was an amalgam of Jeffersonian idealism and Yankee practicality. He would simply move the immigrant directly to the country. While hardly an ardent assimilationist, Page did believe that given time and the proper exposure to American ideas and values, even the less desirable racial types could be assimilated. However, what was a desirable immigrant as opposed to an undesirable one was not always entirely clear.

For example, because of his view that there was plenty of room outside of the cities, Page had no objection to additional settlers. Even the increased volume of immigration did not concern him greatly. Rather, it was that "many of the immigrants that are now coming to us ought to be excluded for lack of character and fitness for citizenship.... We can afford heartily to welcome the strong and the economically independent." But the laws did not keep out many of the unfit.[21] Despite this flood of weaker racial types, especially of the least moral and useful of the less desirable immigrant stock, Page had a place for them; the countryside.

Among its other virtues, the American frontier was seen to have certain restorative powers. The Governor of Minnesota, John A. Johnson, wrote in a 1908 article that the Minnesota countryside had rescued the Scandinavian peoples from "the dull life that had been lived by their peasant forbearers for a thousand years." The author's belief in power of the environment to direct the total development of people was quite strong. He noted that the "alien breeds" from South and Eastern Europe had not sought out Minnesota, which had so readily assimilated such groups as Swedes, Norwegians, Germans, Canadians, Englishmen, and Irishmen into the "American types." The obvious conclusion was that the remarkable powers of the frontier, great though they were, could not prevail to assimilate the unassimilable.[22]

Page, however, had faith in the countryside as both the carrier of virtue and as the creator of economic self-sufficiency. He believed that the value structure of American rural life would lead to assimilation of immigrant cultures faster and more effectively than any other set of surroundings. Conversely, he shared the Progressive belief that the immigrant in the city only aided "boss" control, and that decent municipal government could not take place until the immigrant "power base" was broken. As it was also widely believed that slums were the creation of immigrants simply duplicating the conditions of living they had left in Europe, getting them out of tenement housing into the countryside would improve their health, morals and potential for assimilation.[23]

The irony of immigration between 1895 and 1910 was that so many of the immigrants were from rural backgrounds but had neither the money nor the connections to move directly to farm areas. Page wrote, in an 1911 editorial:

> More than a million immigrants came into the United States in 1910, and 300,000 of them registered their previous occupation as farmers or farm laborers. Yet of this 300,000, less than 50,000 seem to have found their way to the great agricultural states. Many of these men who can till the soil drift into city cellars and hovels from which they emerge to pick up odd jobs. They would like to go on the land and the land needs them.[24]

Page was one of very few prominent editors to support the idea of settling immigrants directly in western areas. He continued to hope that some agency, public or private, would undertake to promote the immigration of city populations, especially of the new immigrants, to the western and underpopulated areas. He did not actually envision this as the business of government, but of some agency of private capital or philanthropy.[25] As an example, he cited the success of the Canadian Pacific Railroad in attracting some 80,000 American farmers onto western Canadian lands. This had been accomplished without any sort of government help.

Of course, certain immigrants in the American past, notably the Swedes and Norwegians, had been brought by the northern railroads en masse to settle the right of way in Minnesota, Wisconsin and the Dakotas. But that day was long past. Now, other agencies or groups would have to take up the slack, and Page publicized the efforts of those who tried.[26]

Page, however, was forced to wrestle with the problems posed by such immigration resettlement activities. Some of the experiments he exhibited in The World's Work were collectivist, a principle he basically abhorred but did accept for agricultural purposes.

Also, despite the magazine's positive view of getting immigrants to the countryside, they were still immigrants, and thus there were numerous qualifications of the abilities and potentialities of the immigrants because of their racial characteristics.

The potentiality for contradiction in the Progressive attitude toward immigration was immense. Page, despite his generally consistent intellectual position on other topics, shared the general confusion and inconsistency which surrounded immigration. His position depended upon which aspect of the problem he was addressing. For example, from the standpoint of assimilability, the Italian was less desirable than the Teutonic or Anglo-Saxon races. However, when the Italians became an economic asset, as when they were injected into the Southern economy, Page could and did actively promote their immigration to the South.[27] In general, where there was a need for labor, racial nationalism and economic nationalism tended to conflict, with the latter overpowering the former. In this area, Page seemed to be more concerned with economic nationalism than with the racial inferiority of the European immigrant. Indeed, the larger problem of white supremacy tended to blur the lines of racial distinction between white men. For example, the need for labor in the Northwestern part of the United States could be dealt with by encouraging immigration of European peoples directly to the areas of greatest need. Page noted that the result would be a leveling of population between Europe and America, leading to greater working efficiency for both areas, and better wages for all. The ultimate result would be to "lift the level of life in all the white man's world."[28]

A more standard view, containing the inherent contradiction of Progressive thought, was found in The World's Work for September, 1907. The article pointed out that certain communities in the Northwest, having driven out Chinese labor in the 1880's, now wished to have them back. The labor unions, despite any direct competition from the Chinese, did their best to inhibit Chinese re-entry. The result was a flood of immigrants from Southern Europe and the Balkans which did not please the natives of the Northwest. The author did not believe these types capable of assimilation by an Anglo-Saxon country.[29]

Another aspect of the economic problem posed by immigrants was their removal of wealth from the United

States. This was occasionally cited as a reason for increased restriction of immigration. One 1911 article in The World's Work indicated that fully 40% of those who currently emigrated to the U.S. intended to return to their homelands with their savings. They also constituted a threat with their willingness to live in overcrowded conditions and accept lower wages. Some 73% of the immigrants were men who crowded into unsanitary living quarters in order to save money. The immigrant, according to the author, resisted unionization by "reasonable and honorable" trade unions, and thus weakened the general position of American labor. "The standard of living," Page wrote, "in several of our basic industries is being lowered by the inthronging immigrants, and the lowering of the standard of these industries has a tendency to depress the standard throughout the country." The author, a professor of Political Economy and Politics at Cornell, had served as a member of the United States Immigration Commission, and quoted portions of their report. He admitted that the major subject of the Commission's inquiry had been the economic aspects of immigration, especially "the immigration of laborers of low standards and efficiency, who imperil the American standard of wages and conditions of employment."

Yet, where previously immigrants of "our own race" or with "our ideals" were assimilated without any lowering of the standard of living, the present tide was too numerically great for easy assimilation. The same article stated that those who immigrate should be interested in permanent settlement, and "take a personal interest in the country." Those who come to work, with the firm intention of returning to Europe, should be discouraged from entering. They took approximately $300,000,000 out of the country yearly. It was the government's duty to "check the incoming tide until our need will care for the immigrant at wages and under working conditions that will raise rather than lower our standard of living."

Finally, the author laid at the feet of immigration some of the economic problems which were indigenous to American economic society. For example, the twelve-hour day and seven-day week of Bethlehem Steel Company was attributed to the desire of immigrants to work long hours in order to save as much as possible. "The superintendent of mills," the author wrote, "showed to investigators lists of hundreds of names of employees who, to increase their earnings and the savings which they might take abroad, had asked to be put on the 12-hour shift and were waiting for the blessed opportunity of a 7-day week."[30] Similarly, the excess of immigrant labor in Pennsylvania coal mining areas supposedly forced lower wages, thus lowering the standard of living. That low wage conditions both pre-existed and survived the high tide of immigration was not clear in 1911. Even Page, however, noted that immigrants tended to return to Europe during periods of economic depression, a fact which should have alleviated downward wage pressure. One ought to have been able to expect a more sophisticated argument from a profes-sor of Political Economy at Cornell University. His slavish adherence to the law of supply and demand as applied to labor, however, offered some indication that economic thought, in 1911, had not progressed much beyond the 1790's.

Page, too, commented upon the cross-migration of immigrant labor, but took a more positive view. He noted that of the one million immigrants who came to the United States in 1907, nearly half returned to their homelands when economic conditions became intol-erable. There was, of course, an adverse monetary flow from the U.S. back to Europe, but he saw this as basi-cally incidental, and as benefiting Europe much more than it hurt the U.S. economy.[31]

Perhaps the most incomprehensible set of conflicts between Page's economic nationalism and his racial nationalism occurred in his handling of the question of oriental immigration. On the one hand, Page appreci-ated the need for labor on the West Coast, a need which impelled the California Fruit Growers Association, in 1907, to call for a relaxation of the Chinese Exclusion Act.[32] On the other hand, there was the basic racial problem. Complicating the unassimilability of the Oriental races was the fact that there were two major and distinct "national-racial-oriental" types, the Japanese and the Chinese. The latter were, given the nature of their political and economic status in the world, not worthy of consideration. The Japanese, however, because of their military and commercial suc-cesses, had forced consideration of their national aims in Asia. Page might admire the Japanese, but he never considered them equal to Anglo-Saxon-Teutonic peoples. He could not, however, blink away the Japanese victory in the Russo-Japanese War.

Page's comments upon the Pacific situation display

his continual equivocation between economic considerations and national-racial considerations. He viewed the Russo-Japanese War as a struggle for control of the Chinese market, and the ultimate control of the Manchurian and Korean areas. Page favored Japan, believing that it would be in the American interest "since the Japanese trade policy is much more liberal than the Russians, it is natural that the commercial interests of the United States should give their sympathies to Japan."[33] When, in mid-1908, it appeared that Japan might seek to restrict Western trade, Page became editorially bitter. He reported a growing dislike of Japanese actions in excluding Western trade from the areas of China and Manchuria under Japanese control. Page conceded that the Japanese had won the right to develop Manchuria, but not to politically control the area or exclude other nations from trading there. Following the Russo-Japanese War, the Japanese had quickly saturated the Korean and Manchurian markets with their goods. The major American exports to these areas consisted mostly of heavy equipment, and despite Japanese domination of consumer trade, they also disregarded basic "trade rights" by copying and selling American and European goods cheaply.[34] "In the final summing up," Page wrote, "all the world will perhaps learn that something more than cleverness and ingenuity and adaptability are required before a nation can rank among the great powers."[35]

Despite his concern about American trade rights in Asia, Page expressed continual admiration for the Japanese. He also favored restriction rather than total exclusion of both Chinese and Japanese immigrants as being the best answer to the West Coast labor shortage. Linking Oriental immigration with the total immigration problem, Page stated that "the opinion is fast gaining ground that immigration from Asia is only a part of our general immigration problem, and should be so dealt with."[36] However, wishing could not make it so.

In a September, 1905 editorial, Page stressed that Chinese labor would not be in competition with white American labor, and simple economic necessity dictated flexibility on immigration policy.[37] He expanded upon this position in a February, 1906 editorial, pointing out that much of the agitation against both immigration from the Orient and from Europe came from labor union leaders. Page maintained that, first, this "low priced labor" soon became "high priced labor," and second, that attempts to shut off foreign labor would drive

American capital to Europe where it would go further in the labor market. In Page's mind, the connection between immigration policy and American economic nationalism was unquestionable. This argument, however, was structured for European immigrants, and despite his belief that restricted oriental immigration was economically useful, he had real difficulties reconciling oriental immigration with his generally stated policy that America should retain an open door policy to assimilable peoples. "The exclusion of the Chinese," he wrote,

> brings in another principle. The
> unnecessary and discourteously harsh
> law against their coming was enacted
> in response to the demands of California
> labor leaders; but a limitation of immi-
> gration from Asia is approved by the
> public sentiment of the country. Still,
> no limitation--not even this--is defen-
> sible on merely personal grounds. If
> you ask whether as an individual a
> Chinese coolie be not entitled to as
> courteous treatment as a Russian Jew or
> an Italian peasant, you must confess that
> he is. But a national policy of immi-
> gration cannot be based on merely per-
> sonal courtesy. It must be based on the
> preservation of the economic and polit-
> ical health of the people. Unrestricted
> coolie immigration would do violence to
> this economic and political health.[38]

What is missing from this statement is as telling as what it contains. No mention of assimilability. For "public sentiment" read racial beliefs, for "economic and political control" read a fear of the undercutting of American wages and potential loss of the political control necessary to maintain social superiority.

There really wasn't any way for Page, or for any of the Progressives, to safely link Oriental immigration with European immigration. Thus, he opted for a general policy of immigration restriction which would open up some possibilities for limited Oriental immigration to the West Coast strictly for labor purposes. However, because there was strong opposition to even this potentially useful aspect of immigration, he did not push the point after 1906. Instead, Page tried to take a larger view, to look to the larger national

ramifications of our Oriental immigration policy.
There is no question that while he believed the total
exclusion policy to be short-sighted, he did not desire,
or even believe in the possibility of the racial assimilation of the oriental peoples into the American
mainstream.

Page's delicacy toward Oriental immigration was
due to his economic nationalism. Page was concerned
with American trade in the Orient, and had noted
editorially that our policy of total exclusion of Chinese immigrants in 1882 had led to an economic boycott
of American goods in China.[39] As we were doing a considerable amount of business with Japan, their feelings
also had to be properly considered. Page, who had
avoided the use of the words "race" or "racial" in editorial comment on Oriental immigration until 1908,
noted in January of that year that the Japanese had
shown "singular wisdom and forebearance in voluntarily
restricting the flow of laborers to the United States."
In a rare moment, he noted also that the "sting of race
prejudice" underlay East-West relations, despite the
Anglo-Saxon admiration for Japanese leadership and
achievements.[40]

Page attempted to educate his readership as to the
proper relationship between the United States and Japan
by soliciting articles from those who understood it
best. Mary Crawford Fraser, wife of the former ambassador to Japan, contributed an article to The World's
Work. So did the retiring Japanese Ambassador to the
United States, Viscount S. Aoki. Both commented upon
the basic friendship between the United States and
Japan, and stressed that their mutual interests would
best be served by avoiding an insulting immigration
policy.[41]

Viscount Aoki's article put the relationship into
perspective. He pointed out that immigration was the
only discordant note in the concert of interests between Japan and the United States. If the United
States were to formalize the problem by passing
Exclusion Laws, "it would be a slap in the face which
no first-class power could permit to pass unnoticed."
Instead, Aoki called for retention of the status quo,
in which the Japanese government would continue to
voluntarily restrict the emigration of laborers to
America. In return, Aoki called for American invest-
ments in Japan, Korea and Manchuria.

The Japanese government was apparently willing to ignore American racism in favor of economic considerations, both present and future. Earlier, the Japanese War loan had been subscribed by American bankers, and Japan's economic stability was partially dependent upon American good will. It was indeed an economic question for Japanese leadership, and their resentment of Western racial prejudice was down-played whenever necessary.

In April of 1909, Page printed an article by the editor of The Far East which spelled out Japan's need for American understanding of Japan's position in Manchuria and Korea, and its continuing concern with American friendship. In the view of the author, Japan was unconcerned over the potential deprivation of Japanese in California of property, or even life. "Everything in life," wrote the author, "is comparative....what would be even the violent death of a few working people in California and the loss of a proprietary interest in real estate" compared to the retention of the broad and official friendship of America toward Japanese interests in Asia?"[42]

In the same April, 1909 issue of The World's Work, Page took pains to reiterate that the West Coast really had no problem with Japanese immigration in any sizeable numbers. However, in order to keep from needlessly insulting the Japanese, the West Coast people should couch their anti-immigration statements in terms and legislation applicable to all immigration. The key to Page's position was the statement that "no sensitive people would willingly submit to direct discrimination against them," but as long as this discrimination was universal against all non-Anglo-Saxon races, how could any complain?[43]

Through The World's Work, Page managed to express conflicting impressions of the economic danger which the Japanese laborer constituted. One author concluded that the highly efficient Japanese had taken over the bulk of the truck gardening, landscape gardening and other service industries on the West Coast, forcing out white competition by lower prices.[44] Another author, after a personal tour of Japan, took the position that Japan's "cheap labor" was an illusion, especially because it took several Japanese to produce, with machinery, the same amount as one white European or American workman. The article pointed to both the inefficiency and the lower standard of living of the Japanese workman, and conveyed indirectly the message that such labor could not really be an asset or a danger to the American West Coast.[45]

Page's equivocation on Oriental immigration, in the final analysis, was based partly upon his economic nationalism, e.g., the need for cheap labor on the West Coast, and partly upon the disconcerting failure of the Japanese to act like an inferior race. For Page, Japan appeared to be a potential market for American manufactures and foodstuffs. He respected ambitious, hard-driving commercial activity, and found himself in the embarrassing position of taking Japan to task for activities which he basically applauded in American entrepreneurs.

Thus, his outburst in 1908 concerning Japanese control of the Korean and Manchurian trade lapsed into acceptance. Page noted, in December of 1909, that our "open door" policy in China conflicted with natural Japanese expansion into Korea and Manchuria. This expansion threatened Chinese political, economic and territorial integrity. However, any position taken by the United States was bound to be offensive to one power or the other, and consequently, disruptive of peace in Asia. Page thus advocated the continuation of friendship toward Japan, and the promotion of peaceful economic expansion into Manchuria, while insisting upon the "open door" for all other nations interested in trading in either China or Manchuria.[46]

Page was perhaps more sympathetic to the Japanese than many Americans. He was highly laudatory of the Japanese leadership, especially after their success in the Russo-Japanese war. The lack of a democratic political system led Page to qualify his praise, but he ranked the Japanese, as a national-racial group, well above the Chinese, and far above the black and brown peoples of the world. During The World's Work's coverage of the Russo-Japanese War, Page sided entirely with the Japanese, finding them generally superior to the Russians.[47]

Page also found the Japanese more cooperative on the immigration question. Japan, in seeking American support for its own Asian policy, had voluntarily restricted its emigration to American territory. Where 31,000 Japanese had emigrated in 1907, there were only 3,000 in 1910. Most of the latter number were students, merchants or government officials. Page was pleased that a clause in the United States treaty with Japan "reserving the right" to impose immigration restriction had been removed in the 1911 treaty. The right to restrict immigration was the prerogative of any sovereign state, and thus its inclusion in a treaty was "doubly gratuitous and doubly an insult." Japan's positive response to this gesture, in Page's view, only created a stronger friendship between Japan and the United States, a friendship which would continue as long as Japan continued to voluntarily restrict emigration to American territory, and respect American trade interests in China and Manchuria.[48]

For Page, as for others, the Japanese presented an exception to accepted racial formulations. The powerlessness of most of the black, brown and yellow peoples had made it logical for the white race to exercise domination. However, by embracing Western technology, by its startling victory over a white nation, and through its strong national pride, Japan stood out as a major power. The Japanese accepted the racial insults of the Western nations for obvious political and economic reasons. However, they did so with ill grace, and did their best to exact a price for these insults.

Page's ambivilence in the matter is perhaps best summed up by a statement he made at the beginning of the Russo-Japanese War.

> ...the races that are akin to the
> Japanese have looked to them with
> this ultimate hope--or perhaps with
> some fear....that she should become
> the dominant power among the yellow
> peoples as England and her offspring
> have become the dominant powers in
> the other parts of the world....It
> seemed a sort of race destiny--a fit
> thing to come to pass. China has a
> thousand students in Tokio alone, and
> the Japanese are born nearer to the
> Chinese than any other nation can
> ever come. Japanese influence, if
> it be not repressed or deflected,
> might extend over Siam, Burmah, India,
> Persia....modernizing them, looking
> toward the awakening of Asia to a
> new life under Asiatic leadership.
> Such is the necessary direction of
> Japanese ambition....it would mean
> the rebirth of Asia under the

guidance of a progressive Asiatic
people--a fit thing in human history, proving that decadent races
may rise.[49]

The Japanese, in Page's view, were the premier
sub-race but they weren't white.

However, even being white did not necessarily help.
Page could afford to be sanguine about the Japanese
because they were not immigrating in any significant
numbers. However, his view of the assimilability of the
"new immigration" from Europe changed with time. Before
1903, he had been quite sure that the United States
could absorb the immigrants from Eastern and Southern
Europe. At least he did not see them as a threat to
Anglo-Saxon superiority on the American continent.[50]
By 1910, however, he had become caught up with eugenics
and had begun to realize that the so-called less desirable peoples in America were breeding faster than the
older American stock.

Page had written, in 1903, that there was time to
"shut out the burdensome comers of the Old World; for,
except in the slums of our cities, our population is
yet sufficiently homogenous...except for the Negroes
and the Jews....We are English yet--that is, we are
of the same kindred stocks that went into the making
of the English race."

Page quoted Professor Giddings of Columbia in
claiming that "75% of our foreign born population in
1900 was of Teutonic and Celtic stock--the very same
that made the English....There is an American race,
and it is English by direct descent and by later fusion
of the original races that made the English." Thus it
was a mistake to "talk of the American people as a mis-
cellaneous conglomeration of races." His objection
to the new immigration was "not its volume but the
large part of it that is of other than the Teutonic
and Celtic stocks."[51]

From 1903 until 1912, Page struggled with the
contradictions of the immigration question. He articulated, in The World's Work, a solution to the slum
and "boss" government problem; send the immigrants to
the countryside. Page also continued to believe that
the immigrant had economic value, and as an economic
nationalist, Page wanted the United States to continue
to tap this source of inexpensive labor. It was in the

area of assimilation that Page was most equivocal. He had presumed that through exposure to American values and institutions, the immigrants and especially their children would eventually become assimilated into American society. Many articles and much editorializing in The World's Work supported this belief. However, by 1910, Page no longer accepted the easy assimilability of the new immigration. In an October, 1910 editorial, he wrote:

> With a million immigrants a year (70 percent of them Italians, Slavs, and Jews) with a declining native birthrate, it is a very simple arithmetical problem to figure out how long it will be before the Anglo-Saxon is submerged with his social ideals and his superior civilization--for no one will deny that the descendant of the British immigrant of three hundred years ago, or of the German exile of 1848, or of the Scandinavian of twenty years ago is the superior of the average member of the horde now passing through Ellis Island.[52]

He discussed at some length the suggestion made by English eugenicists that the subsidization of motherhood for the perpetuation of better racial stock would be in the national interest. England was a leader in this field of inquiry, which for political reasons, as well as social, had yet to achieve practicality. Page knew that such an idea would be "a long time working itself out...but a great point" would be "gained for civilization when a nation realizes that its power and happiness depend more upon the quality of its population than upon anything else."[53]

The thrust of his comments upon this occasion concerned the national breeding of better men. However, the urgency of this message was fueled by the high level of undesirable immigration after 1900. A position such as this points up the dilemma of those who believed on the one hand that immigration was necessary to build up the American nation, and recognized on the other hand that there was a potential for the breakdown of Anglo-Saxon civilization in allowing all peoples to come at random.

Restriction was still a possible solution. "There

is still time to assure the continued Anglo-Saxon
ascendency in the United States by restricting immigration," he wrote in 1910. Unfortunately, political
conditions were unfavorable to such a plan. Page
further contended that:

> the worry is not in the fact that the
> original settlers of North America are
> giving way before a darker race, but
> in the fact that, having worked out
> here a higher type of culture and
> morals, they are being supplanted by
> a breed less advanced. This is not
> the path of progress. Civilization
> prefers that the more advanced stock
> multiply the faster. It especially
> demands that the diseased, the in-
> efficient, and the criminal die out.[54]

Eugenic planning was one way to save Anglo-Saxon
civilization. Intelligent restriction was another.
Page proposed yet a third, that being the creation or
continuation of the current economic conditions of life
which would, through the natural workings of competition, tend to eliminate the undesirable elements through
starvation, or drive them back to their homelands. Unfortunately, the more undesirable breeds of immigrants
had shown incredible tenacity in surviving harsh
conditions.

All three of these proposals presumed the natural
superiority of the Anglo-Saxon-Teutonic amalgam over the
so-called inferior races. The idea that these inferior
races, notably the Jew, the Italian, and the Slav, might
have more physical strength and vitality that the Anglo-
Saxon-Teutonic race was simply unacceptable.

Page never commented, in The World's Work or in his
other public statements, on what came to be the final
solution to the immigration problem. Had he conceived
of the quota system which came to pass in the 1920's,
it is highly probable that he would have supported it
as being the best method of rational restriction
possible under the circumstances. Quite possibly, Page
would have sought higher limits than those which were
imposed in 1924 because his economic nationalism would
have dictated that we continue to encourage the best
educated and most highly motivated Europeans to bring
their talents to America. However, for Page as for so
many of the Progressives, the bottom line was race.

The conflict between racial-nationalism and economic nationalism, in Page's mind, made it impossible for him to find a position on immigration which was not inherently self-contradictory.

[1] Edward Lowry, "Americans in the Raw," The World's Work, IV (October, 1902), 2644-55.

[2] James Davenport Whelpley, "International Control of Immigration," The World's Work, VIII (September, 1904), 5254-59. Jacques Barzun, Race: A Study in Superstition (New York, 1965), revised from the 1937 edition, pp. 50, 55, 183-239.

[3] Kate Holladay Claghorn, "The Changing Nature of Immigration," The World's Work, I (February, 1901), 381-387.

[4] Walter Hines Page, "The Secret of American Expansion," The World's Work, III (January, 1902), 1576.

[5] Walter Hines Page, "The Growth and Migration of the English," The World's Work, II (August, 1901), 1120-21.

[6] Kate Holladay Claghorn, "The Changing Nature of Immigration," The World's Work, I (February, 1901), 381-387.

[7] Hutchins Hapgood, "The Rise of the Russian Jew," The World's Work, I (April, 1901), 589-598. See also Walter Hines Page, "American Society in the Making," IV (September, 1902), 2481-82; Ezra S. Brudno, "The Emigrant Jews at Home," The World's Work, VII (February, 1904), 4471-79; "The Russian Jew Americanized," VII (March, 1904), 4555-67; A. R. Dugmore, "New Citizens for the Republic," The World's Work, V (April, 1903), 3323-36; Major W. Evans Gordon, M.P., [Member of the Royal Commission on Alien Immigration] "Whence Come Our Immigrants," The World's Work, V (April, 1903), 3276-81.

[8] Walter Hines Page, "The Jew in the Republic," The World's Work, IV (October, 1902), 2592-93.

[9] Frederick B. Weaver, "Walter Hines Page and the Progressive Mood," unpublished doctoral dissertation, (University of North Carolina, Chapel Hill, 1956), pp. 103-104.

[10] Walter Hines Page to Charles F. Thwing, President

of Western Reserve University, April 27, 1895, Page MSS, Harvard, cited in Ibid.

[11]Walter Hines Page to Horace Scudder, July 9, 1895, Page MSS, Harvard, cited in Ibid., p. 107.

[12]Walter Hines Page, "A Wholesome Word to the World," The World's Work, V (November, 1902), 2707-08.

[13]Ezra S. Brudno, "The Emigrant Jews at Home," The World's Work, VII (February, 1904), 4471-79; "The Russian Jew Americanized," VII (March, 1904), 4555-67.

[14]See note 3. above.

[15]Walter Hines Page, "Unprecedented Immigration and its Character," The World's Work, VI (May, 1903), 3388-89.

[16]Walter Hines Page, "Immigration and the Purity of the American Race," The World's Work, VI (August, 1903), 3716-17.

[17]Walter Hines Page, "The Massacre of Jews in Russia," The World's Work, VI (July, 1903), 3597-98.

[18]Walter Hines Page, "The Grave Problem of Jewish Immigration," The World's Work, VI (July, 1903), 3598-3601; Walter Hines Page, "The Unbridled Savagery in Russia," The World's Work, XI (November, 1905), 6920-21.

[19]Walter Hines Page, "The Jews in the United States," The World's Work, XI (January, 1906), 7030-31.

[20]Walter Hines Page, "The Burden of the New Immigration," The World's Work, VI (July, 1903), 3601, 3603.

[21]Walter Hines Page, "Immigration and the Purity of the American Race," The World's Work, VI (August, 1903), 3616-17.

[22]John A. Johnson, [Governor of Minnesota] "Fifty Years of an American Commonwealth," The World's Work, XVI (October, 1908), 10820-24.

[23]Claude H. Miller, "The Menace of Crowded Cities," The World's Work, XVI (May, 1908), 10268-72.

[24]Walter Hines Page, "A New Kind of National Conference," The World's Work, XXIII (November, 1911), 15-16.

[25] Walter Hines Page, "The Tide of Immigration," The World's Work, XVIII (August, 1909), 11869-70.

[26] Robert W. Vincent, "Successful Immigrants in the South," The World's Work, XVII (November, 1908), 10908-11; Anita Moore, "A Safe Way to Get on the Soil," The World's Work, XXIV (June, 1912), 215-219; See also, Walter Hines Page, "Public Bodies as Real Estate Agents," XXV (December, 1912), 146-147.

[27] [Staff], "Immigration to the South," The World's Work, XIV (June, 1907), 8959-60.

[28] Walter Hines Page, "The Distribution of White Men," The World's Work, XIV (October, 1907), 9395-96.

[29] F. G. Moorhead, "The Foreign Invasion of the Northwest," The World's Work, XV (March, 1908), 9992-97.

[30] Jeremiah W. Jenks, "The Urgent Immigration Problem," The World's Work, XXII (May, 1911), 14368-74.

[31] Walter Hines Page, "Cross-Currents of Migration," The World's Work, XV (January, 1908), 9732-33; Lewis E. MacBrayne, "How Immigrants Solve the Cost of Living," The World's Work, XIX (April, 1910), 12813-15.

[32] Walter Hines Page, "The San Francisco Schools' Real Issue," The World's Work, XIII (February, 1907), 8491.

[33] Walter Hines Page, "The Russian Danger to Peace in Asia," The World's Work, VI (June, 1903), 3493-94; Walter Hines Page, "Russia or Japan to Control in Asia," The World's Work, VI (June, 1903), 3494-95; Walter Hines Page, "Reasons for Sympathy with Japan," The World's Work, VII (March, 1904), 4496, 4499; Baron Kentaro Keneko, "The Far East After the War," IX (February, 1905), 5868-71; Robert E. Speer, "Korea, Japan, and Russia," VII (March, 1904), 4514-25.

[34] Walter Hines Page, "Our Trade in the Orient," The World's Work, XVIII (June, 1909), 11641-42.

[35] Walter Hines Page, "China versus Japan," The World's Work, XVI (June, 1908), 10305-06. From April to June of 1908, The World's Work took a hard editorial line toward Japan's expansionist policies, which appeared to operate to the detriment of western trade. The April editorial does not appear to be Page's style.

The June editorial, however, definitely is.

[36] Walter Hines Page, "The Chinese and We," The World's Work, X (September, 1905), 6579; Walter Hines Page, "Shall Japanese Immigrants Be Excluded," X (July, 1905), 6343.

[37] Walter Hines Page, "The Chinese and We," The World's Work, X (September, 1905), 6579.

[38] Walter Hines Page, "The Open Door to Newcomers," The World's Work, XI (February, 1906), 7140.

[39] Walter Hines Page, "The Chinese and We," The World's Work, X (September, 1905), 6579; Walter Hines Page, "Shall Japanese Immigrants be Excluded," X (July, 1905), 6343.

[40] Walter Hines Page, "The Sting of Prejudice Against Japan," The World's Work, XV (January, 1908), 9732.

[41] Mary Crawford Fraser, [author of A Diplomat's Wife in Japan and long a resident of that country] "Our Relations with Japan," The World's Work, XIV (May, 1907), 8919-22; Viscount S. Aoki, [retiring Japanese Ambassador] "Japanese Immigration," The World's Work, XV (March, 1908), 10041-44.

[42] Adachi Kinnosuke, [editor of The Far East] "Does Japanese Trade Endanger the Peace of Asia?" The World's Work, XVII (April, 1909), 11463-67.

[43] Walter Hines Page, "The Recurring Japanese Trouble in California," The World's Work, XVII (April, 1909), 11421.

[44] William Thornton Prosser, "A Western View of the Japanese," The World's Work, XVII (December, 1908), 10989-91.

[45] Clarence Poe, "The Bogey of Japanese Trade," The World's Work, XXI (April, 1911), 14209-21.

[46] Walter Hines Page, "Korea-The Passing of a Nation," The World's Work, XX (October, 1910), 13473-74; T. Iyenaga, [Professorial lecturer in the University of Chicago] "Manchuria's Strategic Railroad," The World's Work, XX (June, 1910), 13019-28; Walter Hines Page, "The Japanese Bogey," The World's Work, XXI (March, 1911), 10476-77; David Starr Jordan, "The

Perennial Bogey of War," XXV (December, 1912, 191-196.

[47]Walter Hines Page, "Reason for Sympathy with Japan," The World's Work, VII (March, 1904), 4496, 4499.

[48]William Bayard Hale, "A Chance for Statesmanship," The World's Work, XXI (December, 1910), 13801-06; Walter Hines Page, "An Act of Statesmanship," XXI (April, 1911), 14188. See also Walter Hines Page, "The Japanese and the Pacific," XXII (June, 1911), 14439; and, Walter Hines Page, "A Flock of Old War Bogies," XIV (June, 1912), 132-133 on this theme.

[49]Walter Hines Page, [untitled comments in "The March of Events"] The World's Work, VII (March, 1904), 4495.

[50]See Footnote #5.

[51]Walter Hines Page, "Immigration and the Purity of the American Race," The World's Work, VI (August, 1903), 3616-17.

[52]Walter Hines Page, "Husbanding the Nation's Manhood," The World's Work, XX (October, 1910), 13470-71.

[53]Ibid. Author's emphasis. See also Raymond Pearl, "Breeding Better Men," The World's Work, XV (January, 1908), 9819-24.

[54]Walter Hines Page, "Husbanding the Nation's Manhood," The World's Work, XX (October, 1910), 13470-71.

CHAPTER V

WALTER HINES PAGE AND THE
PROBLEM OF NEGRO IMPROVEMENT

The chronicle of Walter Hines Page's efforts to improve the position of the American Negro is one of frustration and paradox: Frustration insofar as neither Page nor the men with whom he worked were able to overcome the forces promoting white supremacy; paradoxical because Page and his fellow reformers themselves accepted the inferiority of the Negro.

Negro improvement was by no means the only cause which Page espoused during his career as editor and publisher, but it was the one to which he devoted the majority of his time and attention. Almost his entire life, Page was concerned with the problems of the post-Reconstruction South. Although he was born and raised in North Carolina, he was "intellectually a Nationalist...spiritually a Southerner."[1] As an editor, he promoted American nationalism, and Anglo-Saxon superiority. As a nationalist, his primary concern was to build up the South economically and bring it into the mainstream of American economic and social life. Page rejected the continuing Southern sectional attitude, an attitude he described as having been caused by the one great economic error [slavery] and perpetuated by the myth of the lost cause. Further complicating the Southern attitude was the presence of the inferior Negro. While acknowledging the Negro's inferiority, Page saw clearly that without some improvement in the Negro's educational and economic position, the South was doomed to eternal second-rate sectionalism.

The problem was just how much Negro improvement was desirable: certainly not to a level of economic and social equality with whites. Rather, what Page sought was a level of training which would make the Negro useful to the South, not an education which would create Negro dissatisfaction. Even this limited view of Negro improvement was considered dangerous by the Southern advocates of white supremacy.

In point of fact, the presence of the Negro in the South inhibited education in general. Many campaigns for state-supported public schools had been

thwarted by the fear of educating the Negro. As an ex-
patriate Southerner, and an important editor and publisher, Page was an ideal choice for memberships in
organizations which were concerned with Southern education. In 1901, he was invited to join the Southern
Education Board, and later became a member of the
Rockefeller-funded General Education Board, the Slater
Fund and the Peabody Fund Board. In 1907 he became a
member of the Jeanes Fund for Negro Education, despite
personal doubts as to the advisability of being closely
identified with Negro education.[2]

The various boards, which were comprised of both
Northern philanthropists and top Southern educators,
initially expressed interest in Negro education. By
1901, however--indeed, during the first conference of
the Southern Education Board--they found themselves
stymied by Southern intransigence. This necessitated
a shift in policy, away from specific concern with
Negro education toward the concept of universal education. While this meant an attempt to educate both
whites and blacks, whites would be first and receive
a higher level of education. Like Booker T. Washington, in his famous Atlanta compromise speech, the
boards acquiesced in the fact that even though the
South was dependent upon Negro labor, it could not
accept the elevation of that labor.[3]

After his acceptance, in 1901, of a Vice-Presi-
dency on the Southern Education Board, Page followed
the general line of the board in his editorial
activities. He played down the "Negro problem," and
chided those who sought to use that gambit for
political ends. His editorials in The World's Work
mentioned the Negro rarely, and then only in conjunction with the ideal of universal education. His more
pointed articles on Negro education appeared in publications such as The Atlantic Monthly.[4]

In his recent biography of Walter Page,
John Cooper takes a positive view of the Southern Education Board's move from an interest in Negro education
toward universal education in the South. According to
this version, Board President Robert C. Ogden's initial
interest in Negro education had, during the late 1890's
shifted toward "a broader attack on Southern
problems."[5] On the other hand, Louis Harlan viewed
the move as a general sell-out. However, the position
taken by another Page scholar, Frederick B. Weaver, is
closest to the point. Weaver denies that the shift

away from Negro education toward "universal education"
was due to the acceptance of the Southern white
supremacy doctrine by the Northern leaders of the movement. Rather, the shift was due to a realistic ap-
praisal of current problems. Education of the whites
seemed more important on the grounds that they would
retain control of public affairs. However, Weaver
admits that "the frequent attribution of innate
superiority to the Caucasian and the advocacy of his
keeping control did not necessarily preclude an
interest in the Negro's education, although it did not
contemplate much beyond equipping him for useful work."
The Southern distrust of Northern philanthropy required
that the Southern Educational Conference avoid the
resistance that a program aimed solely at the Negro
would invite. In Weaver's view, the "great problem of
the South was not simply discrimination but that
ignorance and poverty on which it fed."[6]

The Southern Education Board's view, as it came
into being in 1901, was perhaps wishful thinking. It
was well articulated by J. L. M. Curry, one of the
founding members:

> I hope that out of this meeting will
> grow unity of effort and cooperation
> of forces, both material and moral,
> to uplift and educate both black and
> white. The state schools must do
> this work. We must proceed first to
> provide adequate opportunities for
> the whites. One properly educated
> white man will help to educate a
> dozen Negroes, while an illiterate
> white man will hold many more Negroes
> in the bondage of ignorance and
> degradation...The education of the
> white youth of the South is the
> shortest road to the education of
> the Negro.[7]

Another member of the Board, Governor Charles B.
Aycock of North Carolina, stated:

> The education of the whites will
> precede the education of the Negroes...
> Our purpose is to do our full duty by
> the Negro...He is with us to stay.
> His destiny and ours is so interwoven
> that we cannot help ourselves up

without at the same time helping him.[8]

And Charles Dabney, a Southern educator, pleaded for "justice and common sense in the education of the Negro," but clarified the purpose and limitations of such education. "We must adapt our instruction to his needs, and, above all, give him that agricultural and industrial training which will prepare him to be a self-supporting citizen."[9]

That Page accepted this shift to "Universal education" is not surprising. There was nothing else to do in the face of Southern distrust and Southern insistence on "...native leadership...without outside criticism or interference."[10]

Page was, however, impatient with the arguments that an educated Negro was a danger to white supremacy. In this regard, he editorially opposed Negro disfranchisement because he believed it to be unnecessary. "At no time within a period that living men need concern themselves about," he wrote in early 1901, "will the Negro vote in any considerable numbers. This is the definite and final and deliberate action of the dominant Southern sentiment." Page further pointed to the fact that the removal of the Negro from politics had led to single-party rule and political stagnation. This situation, he suggested, only served the ends of those interests opposed to industrial and educational reforms in the South.[11]

In his statements on Negro disfranchisement, Page showed little concern for the political rights of the Negro. Rather, he saw disfranchisement as removing what little political influence Negroes had exercised since Reconstruction, and the practical effects of this action would be to eliminate the Negro from educational benefits as well. When, in 1901, the State of Virginia proposed to equate school appropriations to the proportion of taxes paid by Negroes and whites, Page reacted in a World's Work editorial: The Virginia Negroes, he stated, constituted one-third of the population, and thus received one-third of the school fund. They paid, however, only one-ninth of the school tax. If this was to become their share of the school fund as well, the result would be tragic. Throwing the "weaker race on its own slender resources for public education," Page wrote, "...denies the state's obligation to the most ignorant and dependent part of the population." The real problem from Page's viewpoint, however, was "...to disfranchise the Negro and to leave him to pay his own school bills--that is to make him forever an incubus on the community, with little hope for him or for the community."[12]

Page's careful statements on the economic benefits of Negro education were consistently misunderstood by Southern critics who believed him to be "soft" on the race issue. Page did discriminate between types of Negroes, stating in a 1901 editorial that "the intelligent and thoughtful Negro...[the Negro who paid his taxes] was not disbarred."[13] Page had also, in the eyes of such Southern critics as Josephus Daniels, associated with Negroes more closely than befitted a Southerner.

Page was, of course, not friends with individual Negroes, but he did have closer contact with important Negroes than social necessity required. He was in constant correspondence with Negro leadership, and in the more congenial surroundings of Saratoga Springs, New York, he deigned to lunch in public with Booker T. Washington. Even President Theodore Roosevelt had received intense criticism for the same action. Page, however, had a long established publisher-author relationship with Washington, and supported Washington's manual-mental educational theories wholeheartedly.[14]

Basically, Page's viewpoint regarding the proper extent of Negro education is quite well illustrated through his attitude toward the proponents of the extremes, Booker T. Washington and W. E. B. DuBois. As associate editor of the <u>Atlantic Monthly</u>, in 1896 Page returned a manuscript to Washington with this notation:

> ...if you will...show in the next part of your article that this principle which has made a success of Tuskegee is really the proper principle for education in the whole South without reference to race--this I am sure will meet a very hearty response, and will throw your work where it properly belongs, among the great forces of our time and not simply the force of the work done at a single institution...I wish to give it [the article] a place of distinction

in the [coming] number...Come in
to see me at any time.[15]

Alternate solutions, especially those which might
produce Negroes educated beyond their social
possibilities, were rejected by Page. To W. E. B.
DuBois, in 1897, Page suggested a visit to Hampton or
Tuskegee for the discovery of:

> ...the concrete material which would
> give you the best opportunity to find
> an expression for the spiritual and
> intellectual aspects of the [Negro]
> problem...suppose you find at these
> places life-stories and human experi-
> ences which illustrate in a striking
> way the lift from the old darkness of
> slavery into the ambitious life of
> American citizenship at the end of
> the 19th century--would not such
> definite experience as this, if
> properly interpreted, really illu-
> minate the whole subject in a way
> that no amount of theory or educa-
> tional discussion or didactic com-
> monplaces could ever illuminate it?[16]

Page recognized the fact that there were a good
many intelligent and talented Negroes, but he also
recognized the realities of white attitudes toward
higher education for the Negro. In a 1903 editorial,
Page wrote: "There is no more pathetic figure in
modern life than the educated and capable Negro of
high character."[17] Such a person could not indulge
in the white man's aspirations, either socially or
politically. Furthermore, the presence of such men
acted as a goad to the Southern conservatives and
gave them a rallying point from which to attack even
the modest training for agriculture and industry that
Page envisioned for the Southern Blacks.

During his thirteen years as editor of
The World's Work, Page printed three articles by
W. E. B. DuBois. Each of these bore little resemblance
to most of DuBois' writings. During 1911, Page equivo-
cated upon a DuBois article on Durham, North Carolina.
He consulted Dr. W. P. Few, the President of Trinity
College, and printed the article only after receiving
assurances from Few that the article "was not an
overstatement of the facts."[18] The article was

finally acceptable to Page because it stressed elements
of Booker T. Washington's beliefs, specifically the
National Negro Business League philosophy, and echoed
Page's emphasis upon the relationship between basic
education and economic prosperity.[19]

Despite his public acceptance of the "universal
education" line, Page privately expressed his concern
that Negro education was losing ground in the South.
To Wycliffe Rose, President of the General Education
Board, Page wrote that there was:

> overwhelming testimony which shows
> that the Negro in some parts of the
> South...does not receive anything
> like a square deal in the distribu-
> tion of public school money...Now
> of course you know I have no
> sentimental stuff in me about the
> Negro, but I have a lot of economic
> stuff in me about the necessity of
> training him.[20]

Page realized that "it would be...a great mistake for
anybody in the North or anybody speaking at a distance
to begin to agitate this subject." Even "Southern men
of influence and character" could not safely speak out
on this problem.[21]

In addition to Southern racism, there was a problem with funding. According to Louis Harlan, money
for education had to come from:

> the self-taxation of a poor people,
> hampered by the inertia of a political
> machine linked with propertied interests
> hostile to taxation. Antagonism be-
> tween the white and Negro masses [was]
> utilized by opponents of increased ex-
> penditure for universal education...
> the desire of the whites for education
> increased the temptation to deprive
> Negro schools of funds at a time when
> Negroes could not even make articulate
> complaint.[22]

Page was tired of the "constant and senseless
criticism directed against men who try to help the
Negro."[23] Consequently, his novel, The Southerner,
was published anonymously in 1909. In this novel,

Page was able to give free rein to his dream of what his home country could become through proper education in the agricultural and industrial arts. However, even from the safety of an anonymous novel, Page expressed the view that Negro education was merely a means to an end. Through the mouth of the novel's main character, Nicholas Worth, Page stated:

> I care nothing for the Negro merely because he is a Negro. I care for him because he is a man--or a child. I prefer to think of people in the Southern States as people--white and black alike--living under certain conditions, which can be made very fortunate and prosperous conditions, rather than about any particular class or race of them...[24]

At one point in the novel, Nicholas Worth had succeeded in improving the local schools in his home town, both Black and white. For the Negroes, he had instituted training in such things as the proper way to plant cotton. Such practical training brought forth a negative response from the Negro community, and Worth had to face a committee of Negro men and women who "'monstrate' him for wastin' o' de chillern's time, larnin' 'em to plant cotton, when dey oughter be larnin' outen a book."[25] In response, Worth pointed out that without proper agricultural training, their children could not "become independent men, to own farms, to grow cotton and to grow it right." By Worth's showing them the error of their desire for higher, therefore useless, education from books, "the tide of Negro opinion was...easily turned. It is a docile race."[26]

Later in the novel, Worth campaigned for the position of State Superintendent of Public Instruction. His platform called for:

> a good common school within the reasonable reach of every child in the state. There must be the same sort of schools for Negroes, too. The only way to make them better is to train them--to teach them the trades, to teach the honour and the necessity of work. The Negro menace is Negro ignorance.[27]

Speaking to Negro audiences during the campaign, Worth pointed out that there was not going to be any form of social equality between whites and Negroes. To white audiences, Worth maintained that the Negro:

> is a burden and a menace unless he is trained. So, too, is the white man. But the Negro is a child in civilization. Let us train him. That is our economic duty, our economic necessity. Let us teach him to be a help, to build up his family life. Let his women alone. Help him. He is docile, grateful, teachable. He is a man...The only way in which the Negro can be a menace to our civilization is by his ignorance.[28]

Despite the contention of Charles Grier Sellers, Page did not believe in either the actuality or the future possibility of Negro equality. Sellers read into Page's desire for Negro education, and one luncheon with Booker T. Washington, a level of acceptance of the Negro which for Page never existed. "Page," wrote Sellers, "faced the problem of the Negro's place in Southern life with great optimism. He [Page] based his attitude on sound democratic doctrine, writing that 'in any proper scheme of education, there are no white men, no black men--only men.'"[29] Sellers was quoting Nicholas Worth in The Southerner. As inspiring as this statement might be, it is not reiterated in any fashion anywhere else in the 424 pages of the novel. Rather, numerous allusions to Negro inferiority, the Negro's place, and Page's personal concept of the necessity of "training" for agricultural and industrial pursuits dominate the novel.

If it is reasonable to assume that an autobiographical novel, published under a pseudonym, contains more of the author's true feelings and beliefs than his signed works, then Page clearly accepted only limited Negro uplift. Furthermore, the statements in the novel are totally consistent with Page's other public and private statements. Considering Page's entire record, it appears to have been a mistake to attribute to Page, as Sellers did, a warm feeling for the Negro on the basis of one statement in his novel which contradicts a lifetime of statements to the contrary. However, Page did not hate the Negro, nor blame him for the

South's problems. Whenever he could, Page went beyond the "universal education" line of the General Education Board in advocating training for the Negro. There is considerable irony in the fact that Page's efforts for the Negro, which caused so much disapprobation to fall upon him, had extreme limitations. He did not believe in higher education for the Negroes, and nothing in his private correspondence or his public statement in The World's Work and elsewhere indicates that he would have pursued such a course even had there been no opposition to it. His acceptance of general Negro inferiority meant that he had also to accept the basis of Southern resistance to Negro uplift, even though he could see that such resistance was economically short sighted.

Essentially, Page's concern was for Southern progress. The Negro, ignorant and untrained, was a roadblock which had to be removed. Page's efforts, personally and editorially, were not motivated by any deep concern for the Negro per se, but were pointed at a different purpose, the rebuilding of the South.

[1] Robert D. W. Conner, "Walter Hines Page," Southern Pioneers in Social Interpretation, ed. Howard W. Odum (Chapel Hill, 1925), pp. 60-61.

[2] Page Diary, May 16, 1907, page MSS, Harvard.

[3] See Louis R. Harlan, Separate and Unequal (Chapel Hill, 1958), pp. 64-65.

[4] Walter Hines Page, "The Rebuilding of Old Commonwealths," The Atlantic Monthly, May, 1902. This article, along with the two speeches entitled "The School That Built a Town" and "The Forgotten Man" were printed by Doubleday, Page and Company in 1902 under the title, The Rebuilding of Old Commonwealths.

[5] John Milton Cooper, Jr., Walter Hines Page: The Southerner as American (Chapel Hill, 1977), p. 207 ff.

[6] Fredrick B. Weaver, "Walter Hines Page and the Progressive Mood," unpublished dissertation (University of North Carolina, Chapel Hill), p. 164.

[7] The Winston-Salem Daily Sentinel, April 19, 1901, quoted in Dumas Malone, Edwin A. Alderman (New York, 1940), p. 134.

[8] New York Herald, April 27, 1901 quoted in Charles William Dabney, Universal Education in the South (Chapel Hill, 1936), II, pp. 46-47.

[9] Charles William Dabney, Universal Education in the South (Chapel Hill, 1936), II, p. 40.

[10] Cooper, Walter Hines Page, p. 208.

[11] Walter Hines Page, "How Negro Disfranchisement Has Worked," The World's Work, I (February, 1901), pp. 361-362.

[12] Walter Hines Page, "A Threatened Danger to Virginia," The World's Work, I (February, 1901), pp. 360-361.

[13] Walter Hines Page, "How Negro Disfranchisement Has

Worked," The World's Work, I (February, 1901) pp. 361-362.

[14]See Cooper, Walter Hines Page, pp. 217-219.

[15]Walter Hines Page to Booker T. Washington, July 15, 1896, Page MSS, Harvard.

[16]Walter Hines Page to W. E. B. DuBois, June 24, 1897, Page MSS, Harvard.

[17]Walter Hines Page, "Deep Waters of the Race Problem," The World's Work, V (January, 1903), p. 2935.

[18]Walter Hines Page to Dr. W. P. Few (President of Trinity College, Durham, North Carolina), March 22, 1911, Page MSS, Perkins Library, Duke University; Dr. W. P. Few to Walter Hines Page, March 25, 1911, Page MSS, Perkins Library, Duke University.

[19]W. E. B. DuBois, "The Upbuilding of Black Durham," The World's Work, XXIII (January, 1912), pp. 334-338.

[20]Walter Hines Page to Wycliffe Rose, February 23, 1919, Page MSS, Harvard.

[21]Ibid.

[22]Harlan, Separate and Unequal, pp. 73-74.

[23]Walter Hines Page to Willa Wilson Page, February 10, 1907, Page MSS, Harvard.

[24]Nicholas Worth (Walter Hines Page), The Southerner (New York, 1909), p. 385.

[25]Ibid., p. 145.

[26]Ibid., p. 146.

[27]Ibid., p. 226.

[28]Ibid., p. 251.

[29]Charles Grier Sellers, "Walter Hines Page and the Spirit of the New South," North Carolina Historical Review, XXIX (October, 1952), p. 485.

CHAPTER VI

WALTER HINES PAGE AND THE "LABOR PROBLEM":
THE DILEMMA OF A MORAL PROGRESSIVE

Students of the Progressive Era are aware that the
Progressive's concept of reform was limited to the
correction of perceived social and political abuses and
did not attempt to initiate significant change in the
economic structure of society. First, the Progressive
reformers faced the entrenched political power of
capitalism which was bound to resist any restrictions
upon its prerogatives. Second, most Progressives shared
the 19th Century Classical Liberal view that the state
had no right to interfere in personal economic affairs
for to do so would restrict personal liberty. This
attitude created a dilemma for the Progressive.

Because of his belief in the virtues of individualism, the Liberal Progressive balked at any form of
coercion. Even such desirable ends as the education of
the total population could not be forced without vio-
lating the right of the individual to free choice. A
great irony lay in the fact that the Progressive
supported the rights of individuals to dispose of their
property without interference, even though this very
privileged had led, through lack of legislative
restrictions, to the domination of the political process
by concentrated capital. This loyalty to unrestricted
economic individualism, to the individual's right of
contract and his right to the direction and enjoyment
of his property without government interference, led to
a philosophical stalemate where economic reforms were
concerned.[1]

The Progressives, therefore, had little to offer
the working man. The Progressives were ideologically
wed to individualism and thus viewed the collectivism
and coercion associated with unionization as anathema.
Because of their established belief patterns, the Progressives continued to be selectively blind to the
differences between economic and political democracy.
They failed to see that which the modern liberal knows:
there can be no political liberty without economic
sufficiency.

For a man like Walter Hines Page, who was both a
believer in individualism and proponent of justice and

117

morality, the labor question presented a real dilemma.
As editor of The World's Work, Page was basically in
the mainstream of contemporary thought. What he wrote
personally, and what his magazine published, was quite
reflective of the controlling belief patterns in the
1900 to 1913 period. Page, a free trader and a Grover
Cleveland Democrat, strongly believed in the dignity of
work. Throughout his life, Page maintained a belief
in open opportunity and in the idea that hard work,
thrift, intelligence and character invariably led to
success. He believed that political democracy was the
basic reason for America's economic strength and that
national economic progress was based on unfettered
individual striving. He also believed that imbalances
in the economic system were natural, inevitable, and
would work themselves out in time. Accordingly, he
decried government intervention in economic areas. The
only exception to his noncompulsory attitudes occurred
when he could clearly see that national necessity
required it. These exceptions were couched in terms of
"public necessity" or "national purpose."

There is no doubt that Page was first and foremost
a champion of business. This was not simply because of
his commitment to business and industrial growth, but
also because of his strong sense of nationalism. He
believed that the superiority of the American nation
depended in great part upon a strong industrial base.
Anything which detracted from the achievement of U.S.
prosperity had, in his view, no place in American life.

While Page could not escape this dilemma posed by
his economic individualism, he sought to take a
position between labor and management. In doing so,
he found himself caught between two definitions of
rights, the legal rights of property and the moral
rights of labor. Although he could not bring himself
to undermine business, he brought forward his personal
concept of justice and fair play. He suggested a
number of "third alternatives" for creating labor
stability, notably the simple expedient of providing
decent working conditions and reasonable wages. He
often expressed concern for the public, all those
people who were affected by labor-management strife,
and lamented that there was no mechanism for dealing
with such strikes. "The public," he wrote, "ought to
have some means of doing for its own protection."[2]
While remaining true to his beliefs in economic
individualism, Page tried to be the friend of the

workingman and the enemy of organized labor at the same time.

For Page, the proper role of labor was simply one of acquiescent support for the national purpose. Labor should be efficient and productive, not disruptive. It should operate within a given place as part of the American industrial system. Apart from this system, it did not, nor should not, have an institutional existence of its own. Page firmly believed that the American workingman was superior to all others. This superiority was due to America's political democracy, which Page equated with opportunity for individual betterment, personal pride, and independence. He could not accept the philosophical basis of unionism; collectivism, coercion, and class thinking. He viewed unions as limiting agencies which robbed the workingman of incentive and kept the best workers at the level of the worst.[3] In this regard, he constantly cited the British labor unions, with their output restrictions and impossible work rules, as being responsible for the decline in Britain's capacity to compete in world markets.

Unions were a fact, but Page accepted this with reluctance. He realized that wages and working conditions were not all they should be, but even so, he had difficulty accepting strikes for higher wages. Strikes solely for union recognition, he rejected completely, as they threatened individual property rights. While he could understand the frustration of low wages leading to strikes, he could not countenance what appeared to be the planned subversion of the right of individual contract. He commented, in July of 1901, that strikes over such matters as union recognition against the open shop adversely affected whatever moral currency the union had, and unnecessarily led to a "loss of work and of profits in a prosperous time."[4] He stressed that it was the prerogative of the employer to raise or lower wages according to business conditions. As a moral example, Page cited a strike for union recognition at an otherwise exemplary company as having no legitimate basis. "The mass of employees," he wrote, "appreciate the excellent conditions of work, and are simply the victims of a minority's arbitrary action. No progress lies in this direction surely."[5]

The Teamster Union battle for the closed shop, which failed in 1905, gave Page another opportunity to reiterate the idea that the unions were poorly led.

Rather than blame the workingmen, he blamed the
leaders. "The men in many trades," he wrote, "are
waking up to the fact that they have had unworthy
leaders and one of the best results...of the labor
battle...will be a return to sane, constructive union
leadership...Thus, the fight for the open shop,
instead of being destructive, is helping those who are
most vitally affected--the workers."6

The clearest statement of Page's position on the
relative rights of capital and labor came in relation
to the 1901 strike of the Amalgamated Association of
Iron and Steel Workers Union against the newly-formed
United States Steel Corporation. There had been, wrote
Page, "a larger crop than usual of the customary hot-
weather labor troubles."

> But none of these had the signifi-
> cance of the steel strike, in which
> the powerful Amalgamated Association
> tried to wrest from the largest
> combination of capital in the world
> the right to manage its business
> affairs [Author's emphasis]. Had
> it succeeded, a long step would have
> been taken towards the trades-
> unionism which has for years
> throttled English industry, reducing
> labor to a dull, dead level, putting
> a premium on mediocrity, resisting
> to the uttermost the introduction
> of labor-saving machinery and latest
> improvements in manufacturing--by
> which alone can industrial supremacy
> by maintained in these days of world
> competition. It appears clearly that
> the non-union mills of the steel
> corporation in this country are better
> equipped and more economically con-
> ducted than those in which the manage-
> ment has been hampered by the jealous-
> ies and the obstructive policy of
> the labor unions.
>
> Nobody questions nowadays the desira-
> bility of combinations of workmen.
> But if America is to attain the great
> commercial and industrial destiny for
> which she seems marked out, she must
> go into the conflict free from any

hampering restrictions. Most of the
men who are actually managing the vast
steel business today are in these
positions because they have proved
themselves more competent than their
fellows, and stagnation and decay are
the inevitable results of a transfer
of power from the true generals of
industry to less able hands. The
country is to be congratulated,
therefore, that the steel plant
owners have stood firm on this
point, and decisively defeated a
tendency so deplorable in its
effects.[7]

Page did not come to this position automatically.
His ideas were grounded in a Jeffersonian view of
society. He was not an egalitarian, but believed that
men of merit would succeed and the rest would rank
below them in socio-economic classes consistent with
their abilities. He believed that there would always
be social stratification, but no fixed classes. Unlike
Progressives such as Robert La Follette, Page did not
fully believe in the judgment of the people. He
considered it important that society have constructive
management by men who have proven their fitness through
economic success. Actually, he had more faith in the
political judgment of the people than in their economic
judgment.[8]

Page was far more inconsistent in his handling of
the labor question in The World's Work than he was with
any other topic. This was due, in great part, to his
conflicting sympathies. Morally, he believed that
labor was entitled to just wages and reasonable working
conditions, but he did not believe that any agency had
the right to force the property owner to furnish these.
He thus sought to promote justice for labor without in-
terfering with property rights; a frustrating and
basically fruitless endeavor, reflective of both the
liberal dilemma in general and of the failure of
Progressives to fundamentally change economic power
relationships.

Page firmly believed that most labor troubles
could be avoided if employers paid a fair wage. There
was, in his view, a moral imperative that employers
should not pay a wage below subsistence level. On the
other hand, being bound by a "market theory of wages,"

he stipulated that no man should be paid more than he
was worth. "It is not an easy task," he wrote, "to
divide the earnings of industry with ideal justice."[9]
He believed that enterprise, daring and management
ability deserved high reward, but it was impossible to
determine their share of the earnings. Nonetheless,
justice decreed, despite mediocrity and incompetence,
that all who would work should receive a living wage.[10]

Of course, union demands for retention of wage
levels under any and all business conditions were seen
by Page as an artificial barrier to free market
activity. In a 1908 editorial, Page noted that certain
railroad dividends had been too high, and deserved to
be cut. However, he felt that the worker should stand
some of the loss when railroad revenue was down. It
was the unions that required that wages not be cut, and
thus, the railroads were forced to lay off men rather
than keep their work forces at a lower wage. He
concluded:

> The laborer and the investor are
> theoretically partners in the rail-
> road business. They are supposed
> to share alike in the profits of
> good times, and in the losses of
> bad times.

Instead, "the stockholders pay the bill in hard
times,"[11] and for this, Page blamed the unions.

The purchasing power of wages, however, had a lot
to do with the cost of living. In Page's view, labor
was justified in asking for increases when their
wages fell below the cost of living. Unfortunately,
he was never clear on what caused increases in the cost
of living.[12]

Being a free-trader Democrat, he believed that
American industry could compete worldwide without
tariff protection. Supposedly, the increase of foreign-
made goods in the American market would lower prices of
important commodities, and the consumer would benefit.
He was, however, never clear as to whether the lower
profits resulting from lower prices would come from
capital's dividends or from labor's pocket.

Labor's response to such thinking was collective
action. Page's response was more individualism. He
suggested that in a free economy, fixed wages were

unfair. Justice to both labor and capital would be best served by abandoning the fixed wage in favor of piecework rates. The employer would only pay for what he got, and the workingman would have the incentive to produce more. The best workmen would be rewarded, and the worst would likely make enough to survive. The owners of capital would be rewarded with a stable, interested working force. Profits would grow and labor strife would disappear. Such a system, of course, interfered in no way with the prerogatives of ownership. Page made no call for a greater economic share for labor, nor acknowledged any inherent rights to a greater share. He did call for simple justice, and expressed his belief that this was as important to the workingman as gaining a higher wage. [13]

There was yet another party to be considered. It was the public which paid for wage increases through increased prices. "This is proper," Page stated, "provided...that the employing company does not use an increase in wages as a mere excuse to raise the price... At just what point the extra charge on the public becomes unfair...must be determined in every case by the willingness of the public to pay it." [14]

Page had great faith in the public, which he assumed paid close attention to prices. However, he knew that this theory applied only to items of marginal utility. The necessities of life were subject to exorbitant charges, and their prices stood quite free of "the pressure of organized labor." [15] He also knew that wages were not dependent upon prices, that "there is a difference between the price of labor and the price of products." Despite this knowledge, he could lend little positive support to the concept of minimum wage legislation, because it involved coercion. In a 1911 editorial, Page wrote: "The price of labor directly involves human life, especially when wages fail to give subsistence." The police power of government might be invoked to protect human life from starvation wages, but:

> It may as well be confessed that
> the setting of a minimum wage is a
> somewhat dangerous power for the
> state to assume... Yet what are we
> going to do in the presence of such
> facts as every student of our indus-
> trial life knows to exist--in the
> presence of the employment of women

and children, who are economically
helpless, for starvation wages?

Page's solution to this difficulty was to make "such
practices disreputable anywhere it occurs within the
range of your influence. This is the best way, perhaps the only, to a remedy."[16]

Page, however, did not entirely discount the
police powers of the state. He believed that they
could be used to protect citizens against abuses and
act for the benefit of society as a whole when the
basic rights of personal liberty and property were not
infringed upon. In short, where the individual
interest was concerned, the state might not act, but
where the national interest was concerned, it could and
should act. These beliefs led to some blatant equivocation.

For example, Page applauded a Supreme Court decision throwing out the ten-hour-day law in New York
State. He was pleased that the principle of individual
right of contract had been upheld, and noted that the
decision would be "far-reaching in curbing the unreason-
able encroachments upon personal freedom of which union
labor has been guilty."[17] However, he was likewise
pleased that the decision was not rigid. The restriction of hours in occupations which affected public safety, such as railroad employees, might still be declared
constitutional.[18]

In a 1908 editorial, he approved the Supreme
Court's contradictory stance in sustaining the right
of the State of Oregon to limit the working hours of
women. The Court had stated that the weaker sex had to
be protected in situations where men did not. Con-
curring with the Court, Page wrote:

> The decision of the Supreme Court
> sweeps aside this objection (that
> it might, in individual cases be a
> hardship to limit the hours that
> women may work), on the ground that
> such work, even though sought by
> women, is inimical to the best in-
> terests of the race at large. The
> sober common sense of the people
> will approve that ground, and
> applaud the humanitarian spirit of
> the decision, no matter how the

124

advocate of the sweat-shop and the
factory may rail against it.[19]

Page stood squarely on principle where unions were involved, but invoked morality and national necessity to
circumvent his own principles when unions were not
involved.

Another of Page's objections to unions was their
capacity to restrict the training of apprentices. This
interfered with the law of supply and demand, and made
for artificially high wages. The answer, to Page's
mind, was increased industrial education in public
schools. Actually, he believed that standard education
utterly failed to prepare young men and women for business and industrial life. He especially saw the trade
schools as the logical replacement for the union apprentice system, and a way around union restriction of
skilled laborers.[20] Thus, it was with enthusiasm that
he reported in 1912 on the state of Wisconsin's legislative actions "requiring the industrial training of
apprentices and minors between the ages of fourteen and
sixteen to be carried on in 'continuation' schools."
Every town of reasonable size had to provide such
schools. The law further provided protection against
long hours, specified a number of hours which had to be
spent in school at the employer's expense, and required
that training be given in all phases of a trade, a
practice sometimes circumvented by employers which resulted in poorly-trained workmen. Page had often suggested, in The World's Work editorials, the need for
local school districts to make provision for industrial
training.[21] Despite its compulsory nature, Page accepted the Wisconsin plan because such training was for the
greater good of society. It would aid America in its
struggle for commercial supremacy, and would reduce
waste. It also attacked the union apprentice system,
while leaving employers free to decide whether or not
to hire the school-trained apprentices.

Despite his antiunion position, Page consistently
pointed out management abuses. He did indicate that
conditions were, in general, not as bad as claimed by
labor advocates, but he cited consistently in The
World's Work conditions which were substandard or dis-
graceful. Unfortunately, his condemnation of the
abuses of capital was limited to the realm of morality.
Among such mentions was that of the steel industry in
Pittsburgh, especially the subhuman wages and working
conditions of some 300,000 persons. Page pointed out

125

that the wages paid were insufficient to supply the necessities of life, and that the long hours were detrimental to health and safety. On the basis that the steel industry was successful financially, he could see no valid reason for such low wages. In 1912, he wrote:

> This is not an industry of doubtful financial success. It is the very industry, too, in which the system of selling stock to employees on favorable terms has been held up as proof that they are well treated. But, until further facts come out or some change is made, this great corporation will rest under the conviction by public opinion of profiting by ill-paid labor done under unhuman conditions.

Page noted that the 300,000 workers in the steel industry were no longer unionized. It was therefore the responsibility of management to be fair in its dealings with its workers, and the ultimate responsibility of the stockholders to be sure their dividends did not rest on the inhumane treatment of company employees.[22] Such criticisms of capital's abuse of its prerogatives was not infrequent, but was always couched in terms of justice and morality.

In his desire to be fair to unions, Page consistently contradicted himself. On the one hand, he accepted the inevitability of unions, writing in 1902 that:

> Labor unions have come to stay. They will grow rather than diminish... They call for the wisest guidance if they are really to build up the great character of American citizenship while they are struggling merely to gain the strength of compact organization. Every great movement in a democracy must be tested at last by its influence on the individual [Author's emphasis]. The care of classes is the business of older and less efficient social systems. The normal nurture and the free development of the individual is the mark of a democracy.[23]

On the other hand, Page did not accept the inevitability of union coercion and dictation. He sought to
promote a modification of union ideals and purposes
which was conformable to the principles of individualism. Page believed that the proper role of unions was
to operate conservatively, to police unfair management.
They should incorporate, so as to sue and be sued, and
thus take financial responsibility for their actions.
Although he admitted that incorporation by unions had
been avoided because they felt discriminated against
by the courts, he felt that by so doing, unions "would
gain in dignity...and conservative influence... Public
sympathy," he wrote, "is much more ready to be extended
to the laboring man, if he have a good cause, then to
the capitalist."[24]

The real key to union effectiveness was leadership.
Leadership should be conservative, patriotic and re-
strained, or else internal prosperity and international
commercial supremacy would disappear. Noting that
labor unions were organizations for self-protection,
they owed it to themselves to act responsibly. Of
equal importance, it was incumbent upon the managers of
capital to deal squarely with the workman, if reasonable labor-management relations were to be maintained.[25]
Among those cited by Page as being exemplary union
leaders was John Mitchell of the United Mine Workers,
who had consistently been moderate in his demands upon
the mine owners, and had acted to avert strikes for
spurious causes.[26]

A major facet of responsible union leadership, in
Page's view, was the avoidance of political involvement. Labor in politics was synonymous with "class
politics." When, in 1908, Samuel Gompers made an
effort to deliver the labor vote to certain Democratic
Party candidates, Page reacted. In a World's Work
editorial, he wrote:

>   It is a grave misfortune for any
>   industrial or social or other non-
>   political organization to 'go into
>   politics' because such action de-
>   stroys independent individual po-
>   litical freedom. Every man ought
>   to vote as an individual regardless
>   of every consideration but his
>   political convictions.[27]

In a companion article, by Francis John Dyer, The

World's Work pointed out that political activity by trade unions either destroys the trade union, or leads to labor class activity. Whereas the former might have been amenable to Page, the latter definitely was not. The preservation of trade unions, under responsible leadership, was far more acceptable than the creation of a labor party or labor class thinking.[28] In a letter to Dyer, soliciting the article, Page asked whether "it is Gomper's plan, or is there any hope for, or is it anybody's plan again to try to form a separate labor party?"[29] Page totally abhorred the concept of labor as a political class.

Perhaps the ultimate illustration of the paralysis which individualism induced in the Progressives was the problem of child labor. Page discussed this problem from every standpoint but the most logical one. He dwelt upon the economic impracticality of child labor, and the eventual effects on the white population "of a low grade" of the system. It appeared that everyone, the "whole community... the press, the pulpit, the schools, the women in their various clubs... "were on the side of child labor legislation. Only the powerful mill owners were against it.

One strong argument against child labor in the South was the racial appeal. Child labor "threaten[ed]... the supremacy of the white laboring classes over the colored." The Negro sent his child to school; the illiterate white sent his to the cotton mill. Working long hours under poor conditions led to loss of physical stamina and ill health. Children did not get the proper training needed to manufacture the better grades of cotton cloth necessary to meet world competition.

Page believed that public opinion had good effect on regulating economic abuses once it was aroused by publicity. But until it was aroused, "new industrial communities... slip gradually into grave abuses before the public becomes aware of it." Page called child labor a "striking instance of the immorality of organized industry." His objection was stated in moral and economic terms, and he did not suggest legislative relief, pointing out that the public efforts to limit such abuses by government regulation had so far met with limited success.[30]

Child labor was one area which apparently made

Page sufficiently uncomfortable as to cause him to avoid personal comment. He mostly left this topic to other authors, albeit ones which shared his general views. Thus, he allowed equivocation, as in one article which stated that "it is a moral crime to compel a child to work for its sustenance, although much of this work is really given with a philanthropic purpose."[31] Page could only make a moral appeal against child labor or point to the long-term economic effects because legislative restrictions on child labor would be an invasion of individual rights.

Page also struggled with the problem of paternalism, as it was involved in the question of pensions. He supported plans which were based upon workers' contributions, but he flatly denounced plans such as the British old-age pension plan which made the government foot the entire bill.[32] He did not believe that it was the government's responsibility to take care of workers in their old age, but he did feel that government ought to promote thrift and self-sufficiency when possible. The machinery for saving through insurance companies and savings banks was available to workers. Page viewed the workingman's life through middle class eyes, in terms of "accumulating a competence." The quality of life for the workingman, during twenty-five or thirty years of thrift and hard work required to accumulate a competence, was a different problem altogether. In Page's view, for the skilled workman, the opportunity was there, but "whether a larger proportion of workingmen wisely use the machinery of modern life... is impossible to say."[33] It was still the responsibility of the individual to take care of himself.

Another worker incentive plan, profit sharing, invited Page's comment. Page was skeptical of profit sharing plans, but found the concept of employee stock purchase plans acceptable. He published Andrew Carnegie's views that profit sharing would come through stock purchases by employees and, in time, labor would come to own a large portion of the means of production. Such a method would retain incentive while avoiding the obvious pitfalls of socialism, or the undermining of character which would ensue from direct gifts to workmen. The weakness of this plan, naturally, was the fact that ownership of stock required strict savings from already-meager salaries.

The advantages were also clear, and in line with

Page's goal of labor peace. Employee stock purchase plans tended to create a community of interest, tie the worker to the company, and undermine the adversary position of unions. No better methodology could be found to aid the workingman without strengthening the unions. For Page, the promotion of personal incentive was the primary goal. Profit sharing through stock purchase or even through bonuses for superior achievement was a means, not an ideological end in itself. Where the worker could be involved in a "capitalist" relationship with the company which employed him, the result was usually mutually beneficial.[34] The bottom line in Page's sanctioning of direct profit sharing programs was that the worker had to earn his share; he had no right to any such profits unless the company saw fit to reward him.

Walter Hines Page's position on the labor problem was illustrative of the dilemma of the moral Progressive; of the 19th-Century Classical Liberal in a 20th-Century industrial world. He expressed his concern for the rights of individual freedom, with personal incentive and opportunity and with national industrial and commercial supremacy. His concern for justice and fair play for all led him to seek third alternatives which would be equitable for both employer and employee without limiting employer prerogatives. However, he was hampered in this effort by his strong belief in the ethic of individualism, and by the fact that the confrontation between Labor and Capital was indeed one of principle. He accepted the fact that unions were a fact of economic life in America, but he was never reconciled to the collectivist principles upon which unionization was based. He disliked most of all the coercive aspects of unions, even while he recognized that employer oppression was a fact.

In the end he never strayed very far from the position he enunciated in 1907. Writing of a printers' union strike at the Garden City Press of Doubleday, Page and Company, Page stated:

> The owners of this publishing house
> might conceivably shut it up and earn
> their livings in some other way... but,
> as they regard their duty to themselves
> and to society, they could not con-
> ceivably conduct it at the retrogres-
> sive and uneconomic dictation of other
> persons, especially when this dictation

is based on a plan of work that makes
for inefficiency and weakens manhood.[35]

[1]Otis L. Graham, Jr., An Encore for Reform (New York, 1967).

[2]Walter Hines Page, "The Coal Strike and the Public," The World's Work, I (November, 1900), 5.

[3]Walter Hines Page, "Are Our Trade Unions Following the English Example," The World's Work, IV (October, 1902), 2995-96.

[4]Walter Hines Page, "The May Labor Strikes," The World's Work, II (July, 1901), 914.

[5]Walter Hines Page, "A Strike in a Labor Utopia," The World's Work, II (July, 1901), 914-915.

[6]Walter Hines Page, "The Open Shop and New Labor Leadership," The World's Work, XI (December, 1905), 6918; Walter Hines Page, "The Terrific Drain of Labor Wars," VIII (May, 1904), 4732; Walter Hines Page, "The Chicago Strike," X (June, 1905), 6228-29; Walter Hines Page, "The Fight About the 'Open' Shop," IX (January, 1905), 5673.

[7]Walter Hines Page, "The Real Issue of the Strike," The World's Work, II (September, 1901), 1133-34.

[8]Page Diary, May 28, 1907, Page MSS, Harvard.

[9]Walter Hines Page, "Property and Justice," The World's Work, XXII (October, 1911), 14907-08.

[10]Walter Hines Page, "A Corporation's Employees," The World's Work, XXIII (March, 1912), 492-493.

[11]Walter Hines Page, "A Possible Great Railroad Labor War," The World's Work, XVI (August, 1908), 10521-22.

[12]Walter Hines Page, "The Ever-Rising Cost of Living," The World's Work, XIX (January, 1910), 12424-25.

[13]Walter Hines Page, "Scientific Management and the Labor Unions," The World's Work, XXII (May, 1911),

14311; "Humane Conditions of Employment," The World's Work, V (January, 1903), 2936.

[14]Walter Hines Page, "New Ways in Labor Troubles," The World's Work, VI (August, 1903), 3718-19.

[15]Ibid.

[16]Walter Hines Page, "God Help the Helpless! Will You?" The World's Work, XXII (September, 1911), 14796.

[17]Walter Hines Page, "The Ten-Hour Day Unconstitutional," The World's Work, X (June, 1905), 6233; See, also, Walter Hines Page, "One Law for Labor and Capital," The World's Work, XV (March, 1908), 9959-60.

[18]Ibid.

[19]Walter Hines Page, "The Hours of Women's Work," The World's Work, XV (April, 1908), 10063-64. See, also, Walter Hines Page, "The Long Day and a Deep Shame," The World's Work, XII (May, 1906), 7485-85.

[20]Walter Hines Page, "How to Prevent Human Waste," The World's Work, XXIII (March, 1912), 499-500.

[21]Walter Hines Page, "The Need for Vocational Training," The World's Work, XVIII (June, 1909), 11642.

[22]Walter Hines Page, "A Corporation's Employees," The World's Work, XXIII (March, 1912) 492-493.

[23]Walter Hines Page, "The Deep Seriousness of Labor Unions," The World's Work, V (December, 1902) 2820-23.

[24]Walter Hines Page, "The Inherent Weakness of Labor Unions," The World's Work, II (October, 1901), 1246-47.

[25]Walter Hines Page, "Contrasting Types of Labor Leaders," The World's Work, VI (September, 1903), 3835-36; Walter Hines Page, "The Career of a Labor Brigand," VI (October, 1903), 3942-43; See, also, "The Open Shop and New Labor Leadership," The World's Work, XI (December, 1905), 6918.

[26]Walter Hines Page, "The Open Shop and New Labor Leadership," The World's Work, XI (December, 1905), 6918.

[27]Walter Hines Page, "The Labor Vote," The World's

Work, XVI (October, 1908), 10739; See, also, "Labor's Dangerous Part in Politics," The World's Work, XVI (September, 1908), 10629.

[28]Francis John Dyer, "Can 'Labor' Boycott a Political Party?" The World's Work, XVI (October, 1908), 10831-34.

[29]Walter Hines Page to Francis John Dyer, July 14, 1908, Dyer MSS, Bancroft Library, University of California, Berkeley, California.

[30]Walter Hines Page, "A National Movement Against Child Labor," The World's Work, IX (November, 1904), 5456.

[31]Robert Hunter, "The Children Who Toil," The World's Work, XI (December, 1905), 6991-95; Arthur Wilson Page, "The Cotton Mills and the People," The World's Work, XIV (June, 1907), 8990-9002.

[32]Walter Hines Page, "Will England Surrender to Socialism?" The World's Work, XVI (September, 1908), 10636-37; "A Country That Has No Paupers," Ibid., 10637-38; See, also, Walter Hines Page, "Comfort in Old Age by Government Help," XIX (December, 1909), 12313.

[33]Walter Hines Page, "Is Thrift a Lost Virtue?" The World's Work, IV (May, 1902), 2036-37.

[34](Staff) "A Labor Union Turned Capitalist," The World's Work, V (February, 1903), 3140; Walter Hines Page, "A New Kind of Unionism," XVIII (August, 1909), 11868-69.

[35]Walter Hines Page, "The Open Shop--A Case in Point," The World's Work, XIV (August, 1907), 9164-65.

SELECTED BIBLIOGRAPHY

Manuscripts

Francis John Dyer Papers, 1908. Bancroft Library. University of California, Berkeley.

Walter Hines Page Papers, 1880-1918. Houghton Library. Harvard University, Cambridge, Massachusetts.

Walter Hines Page Papers, 1912. Perkins Library. Duke University, Raleigh, North Carolina.

Handbooks and Directories

Ayer, N.W. & Son's Directory of Newspapers and Periodicals. Philadelphia, published annually.

Rowell, George P. Directory of American Periodicals. New York, 1900-1910.

Newspapers

The Winston-Salem Daily Sentinel, 1901. Winston-Salem, North Carolina.

New York Herald, 1901. New York.

Raleigh News and Observer, 1905. Raleigh, North Carolina.

New York Times, 1900. New York.

Periodicals

The Atlantic Monthly, 1902-1907. Boston.

Review of Reviews, 1891. New York.

The World's Work, 1900-1913. New York.

Collected Documents, Letters and Works

Odum, Howard W., ed. Southern Pioneers in Social

Interpretation. Chapel Hill, 1925.

Hazen, Charles Downer, ed. The Letters of William Roscoe Thayer. Boston, 1926.

Thayer, William Roscoe. The Life and Letters of John Hay. Boston, 1915.

The School of Tomorrow. New York, 1911. (A collection of prize essays from The World's Work.)

Reminiscences and Autobiographies

Baker, Ray Stannard. American Chronicle: The Autobiography of Ray Stannard Baker (David Grayson). New York, 1945.

Bok, Edward. The Americanization of Edward Bok. New York, 1921.

Daniels, Josephus. Editor in politics. Chapel Hill, 1941.

_____. Tar Heel Editor. Chapel Hill, 1939.

Doran, George H. Chronicles of Barabbas. New York, 1935.

Marcosson, Isaac F. Adventures in Interviewing. New York, 1920.

_____. "Personal Portraits," The Bookman, XXXVIII (September, 1913), 22-25.

Perry, Bliss. And Gladly Teach: Reminiscences. Boston, 1935.

Sedgwick, Ellery. The Happy Profession. Boston, 1946.

Sinclair, Upton. American Outpost. New York, 1932.

_____. The Autobiography of Upton Sinclair. New York, 1962.

_____. The Brass Check. Pasadena, California, 1920.

Steffens, Joseph Lincoln. The Autobiography of Lincoln Steffens. New York, 1931.

Sullivan, Mark. The Education of an American. New York, 1938.

Tarbell, Ida M. All in the Day's Work. New York, 1939.

Biographies

Blum, John Morton. Woodrow Wilson and the Politics of Morality. Boston, 1956.

Dennett, Tyler. John Hay: From Poetry to Politics. New York, 1933.

Gregory, Ross. Walter Hines Page: Ambassador to the Court of St. James's. Lexington, Kentucky, 1970.

Hendrick, Burton J. The Life and Letters of Walter Hines Page. 3 vols. New York, 1921-25.

_____. The Training of an American. Boston, 1928.

Lyon, Peter J. Success Story: The Life and Times of S.S. McClure. New York, 1963.

Malone, Dumas. Edwin A. Alderman. New York, 1940.

Mims, Edwin. "Walter Hines Page: Friend of the South," The South Atlantic Quarterly, XVIII (April, 1919), 97-115.

Morrison, Joseph L. Josephus Daniels Says... Chapel Hill, 1962.

Mowry, George E. Theodore Roosevelt and the Progressive Movement. Madison, Wisconsin, 1946.

Pringle, Henry. Theodore Roosevelt: A Biography. New York, 1946. (First published in 1931.)

Sedgwick, Ellery. "Walter Hines Page," The World's Work, XXXVII (February, 1919), 375-378.

Sellers, Charles G., Jr. "Walter Hines Page and the Spirit of the New South," North Carolina Historical Review, XXIX (October, 1952), 481-499.

Weaver, Fredrick B. "Walter Hines Page and the Progressive Mood." Unpublished doctoral dissertation,

University of North Carolina, Chapel Hill, 1956.

Monographs and Special Studies

Barzun, Jacques. Race: A Study in Superstition. New York, 1965. (Revised from the 1937 edition.)

Blair, Lewis H. A Southern Prophecy. Boston, 1964. (Reprinted from the original 1889 edition.)

Cash, W.J. The Mind of the South. New York, 1941.

Dabney, Charles William. Universal Education in the South. 2 vols. Chapel Hill, 1936.

Dewey, John. "The Future of Liberalism," Journal of Philosophy, XXXII (April 25, 1935).

Graham, Otis L. An Encore for Reform. New York, 1967.

Grimes, Allen P. The Political Liberalism of the New York Nation - 1865-1932. Chapel Hill, 1953.

Grob, Gerald M. "The Knights of Labor and the Trade Unions, 1878-1886," Journal of Economic History, XVIII (June, 1958), 176-192.

Gross, Gerald, ed. Publishers on Publishing. New York, 1961.

Handlin, Oscar and Mary, "The Origins of the Southern Labor System," William and Mary Quarterly, VII (April, 1950), 219-222.

Handlin, Oscar. The Uprooted. New York, 1951.

Harlan, Louis R. Separate and Unequal: Public School Campaigns and Racism in the Southern Seaboard States 1901-1915. Chapel Hill, 1958.

Hendrick, Burton J. The Age of Big Business. New Haven, 1919.

_____. The Jews in America. New York, 1923.

_____. The Story of Life Insurance. New York, 1907.

Hicks, John B. Populist Revolt. New York, 1931.

Higham, John. Strangers in the Land. New York, 1963.

Hofstadter, Richard. Age of Reform. New York, 1955.

Josephson, Matthew. The Robber Barons. New York, 1934.

Mann, Arthur. Yankee Reformers in the Urban Age. New York, 1966. (Original printing, Boston, 1954.)

May, Henry F. The End of American Innocence. New York, 1959.

McCloskey, Robert Green. American Conservatism in the Age of Enterprise: 1865-1910. Cambridge, Massachusetts, 1951.

Mott, Frank Luther. "Magazines and Books, 1895: A Merging of Two Fields," Journalism Quarterly, XXXII (Winter, 1955), 21-26.

_____. "The Magazine Revolution and Popular Ideas in the Nineties," Proceedings of the American Antiquarian Society, LXIV (April, 1954), 195-214.

Mowrey, George E. The California Progressives. Berkeley, 1951.

Page, Arthur Wilson, et al., ed. The Country Life Press. New York, 1920.

Page, Walter Hines. A Publisher's Confession. New York, 1905.

_____. A Publisher's Confession. New York, 1923. (New edition with an introduction by Frank Nelson Doubleday.)

_____. "Southern Educational Conferences," The Independent, May 15, 1902, pp. 1156-58.

_____. "Southern Opinion of the Race Problem," New York Times, May 27, 1900.

_____. "The Last Hold of the Southern Bully," Forum, XVI (November, 1893), 310-311.

_____. The Rebuilding of Old Commonwealths. Boston, 1902.

Pollack, Norman. The Populist Response to Industrial
     America. New York, 1960.

Woodward, C. Vann. Origins of the New South: 1877-
     1913. Louisiana State University, 1951.

_____. The Strange Career of Jim Crow.
     New York, 1955.

_____. Tom Watson: Agrarian Rebel. New
     York, 1958.

General Works

Bellamy, Edward. Looking Backward: 2000-1887. Boston,
     1966. (First published, 1888.)

Commager, Henry Steele. The American Mind: An Inter-
     pretation. New Haven, 1950.

Croly, Herbert. The Promise of American Life. New
     York, 1912.

Degler, Carl N. Out of Our Past. New York, 1959.

Goldman, Eric F. Rendezvous with Destiny. New York,
     1956.

Hamer, Philip May, ed. A Guide to Archives and Manu-
     scripts in the United States. (U.S. National
     Historical Publications Commission, 1961.)

Hay, John. The Bread-Winners. New York, 1884.

Hays, Samuel P. The Response to Industrialism: 1885-
     1914. Chicago, 1957.

Hofstadter, Richard. American Political Tradition. New
     York, 1948.

Howells, William Dean. A Traveler From Altruria. New
     York, 1957. (First published, 1894.)

Link, Arthur. Wilson: The New Freedom. New Jersey, 1956.

Mann, Arthur, ed. The Progressive Era. New York, 1963.

Mott, Frank Luther. A History of American Magazines. 5 vols. Cambridge, Massachusetts, 1931-57.

Norris, Frank. The Octopus. New York, 1901.

Peterson, Theodore Bernard. Magazines in the Twentieth Century. Champaign, Illinois, 1956.

Wood, James Playsted. Magazines in the United States. New York, 1956. (Original publication, 1949.)

Worth, Nicholas. (Pseudonym for Walter Hines Page) The Southerner. New York, 1909.